Walk in the Light Series

Names

The Father, the Son and the Importance of Names in the Scriptures

Todd D. Bennett

Shema Yisrael Publications

Names
The Father, the Son and the Importance of Names in the Scriptures

Third printing 2012

Unless otherwise noted, Scripture passages are translated by the author.

For information write: Shema Yisrael Publications, 123 Court Street, Herkimer, New York 13350.

ISBN: 0-9768659-2-0
Library of Congress Number: 2005910465

Some illustrations by Gustave Dore used with permission from www.creationism.org.

Printed in the United States of America.

Please visit our website for other titles:
www.shemayisrael.net

For information regarding publicity for author interviews call (315) 939-7940

Names

The Father, the Son and the Importance of Names in the Scriptures

"Who has ascended into heaven, or descended?
Who has gathered the wind in His fists?
Who has bound the waters in a garment?
Who has established all the ends of the earth?
What is His Name, and what is His Son's Name, if you
know?"
Proverbs (Mishle) 30:4

TABLE OF CONTENTS

Acknowledgements

Introduction   i

Chapter 1   In the Beginning   1

Chapter 2   Lost in Translation   5

Chapter 3   The Name of God?   9

Chapter 4   The Lord   16

Chapter 5   The Name of the Father   27

Chapter 6   Pronouncing the Name   34

Chapter 7   The Name in the Scriptures   41

Chapter 8   The Third Commandment   53

Chapter 9   The Name of the Son   59

Chapter 10   Jesus   70

Chapter 11   Messiah and the Name   82

Chapter 12   Christ   87

Chapter 13   Power in the Name   92

Chapter 14   Restoring the Names   99

Chapter 15   In the End   110

Endnotes   115

Appendix A - Hebrew Names of Scriptures

Appendix B - The Walk in the Light Series

Appendix C - The Shema

Appendix D – Shema Yisrael

Acknowledgments

I must first and foremost acknowledge my Creator, Redeemer and Savior who opened my eyes and showed me the Light. He never gave up on me even when, at times, it seemed that I gave up on Him. He is ever patient and truly awesome. His blessings, mercies and love endure forever and my gratitude and thanksgiving cannot be fully expressed in words.

Were it not for the patience, prayers, love and support of my beautiful wife Janet and my extraordinary daughter Morgan I would never have been able to accomplish this work. They gave me the freedom to pursue the vision and dreams that my Heavenly Father placed within me and for that I am so very grateful. I love them both more than they will ever know.

I have also been blessed by the birth of my son, Shemuel, during the completion of this book. His very existence is a witness to the faithfulness of the One I serve and a confirmation of this work by the very meaning of his name.

Loving thanks to my father for his helpful comments and editing and who also tirelessly watched and held down "the fort" while I was away traveling, researching, writing and speaking.

Introduction

"²⁰ Everyone who does evil hates the light, and will not come into the light for fear that his deeds will be exposed. ²¹ But whoever lives by the truth comes into the light, so that it may be seen plainly that what he has done has been done through God."
John 3:20-21 NIV

This book entitled "Names" is part of a larger body of educational work called the "Walk in the Light" series. As such it is built upon a number of other topics and ideally the reader would have read about Paganism in Christianity as well as the need for restoration. Due to the importance of the subject of this text, and each volume in the series, I have attempted to present them in such a fashion that they can stand alone. In order to do this I have used extensive annotations and I would encourage the reader to review the endnotes in order to better understand the present subject and fill in some gaps which may appear in the text.

This book, and the entire series, was written as a result of my search for the truth. Having grown up in a major protestant Christian denomination since I was a small child, I had been steeped in doctrine which often times seemed to contradict the very words contained

within the Scriptures. I always considered myself to be a Christian, although I never took the time to research the origins of Christianity or to understand exactly what the term Christian really meant. I simply grew up believing that Christianity was right and every other religion was wrong or in some way deficient.

Yet, my beliefs were founded on more than simply blind faith. I had experienced a "living God," my life had been transformed by a loving Redeemer and I had been filled with a powerful Spirit. I knew that I was on the right track, but again, I continually felt something was lacking. I was certain that there was something more to this religion called Christianity; not in terms of a different God, but in terms of what composed this belief system to which I subscribed, and this label which I wore like a badge.

Throughout my Christian walk I experienced many highs and some lows, but along the way I never felt like I fully understood what my faith was all about. Sure, I knew that "Jesus died on the cross for my sins" and that I needed to believe in my heart and confess with my mouth in order to "be saved." I "asked Jesus into my heart" when I was a child and sincerely believed in what I had done, but something always felt like it was missing. As I grew older, I found myself progressing through different denominations, each time learning and growing, always adding some pieces to the puzzle, but never seeing the entire picture.

College ministry brought me into contact with the baptism of the Holy Spirit and more charismatic assemblies yet, while these people seemed to practice a more complete faith than those in my previous

denominations, many of my original questions remained unanswered and even more questions arose. It seemed that at each new step in my faith I added a new adjective to the already ambiguous label "Christian." I went from being a mere Christian to a Full Gospel, New Testament, Charismatic, Spirit Filled, Born Again Christian; although I could never get away from the lingering uneasiness that something was still missing.

For instance, when I read Matthew 7:21-23 I always felt uncomfortable. In that Scripture, the Messiah says: *"Not everyone who says to Me, Lord, Lord, will enter the kingdom of heaven, but he who does the will of My Father Who is in heaven. Many will say to Me on that day, Lord, Lord, have we not prophesied in Your name and driven out demons in Your name and done many mighty works in Your name? And then I will say to them openly (publicly), I never knew you; depart from Me, you who act wickedly [disregarding My commands]."* The Amplified Bible.

This passage of Scripture always bothered me because it sounded an awful lot like the modern day Christian Church, in particular, the charismatic churches which I had been attending where the gifts of the Spirit were operating. According to the Scripture passage it was not the people who *believed* in the spiritual manifestations that were being rejected, it was those who were *actually doing* them. I would think that this would give every Christian cause for concern.

First of all "in that day" there are *many* people who will be calling the Messiah "Lord." They will also be performing incredible spiritual feats in His Name. Ultimately though, the Messiah will openly and publicly

tell them to depart from Him. He will tell them that He never knew them and specifically He defines them by their actions, which is the reason for their rejection; they acted wickedly or lawlessly. In short, they disobeyed His commandments. Also, it seems very possible that while they thought they were doing these things in His Name, they were not, because they may have never known His Name. In essence, they did not know Him and He did not know them.

I think that many Christians are haunted by this Scripture because they do not understand who it applies to or what it means. If they were truly honest they must admit that there is no other group on the face of the planet that it can refer to except for the "Christian Church."

Ultimately, my search for answers brought me right back to the starting point of my faith. I was left with the question: "What is the origin and substance of this religion called Christianity?" I was forced to examine the very foundations of my faith and many of the beliefs to which I subscribed and to test them against the truth of the Scriptures.

What I found out was nothing short of earth shattering. I experienced a personal parapettio, which is the moment in Greek tragedies where the hero realizes that everything he knew was wrong. I discovered that many of the foundations of my faith were not rocks of truth, but rather the sands of lies, deception, corruption, tradition and paganism. I saw the Scripture passage in the prophesy of Jeremiah (Yirmeyahu) come true right before my eyes. In many translations, this passage reads: "O LORD, *my strength and my fortress, My refuge in the day of*

affliction, The Gentiles shall come to You from the ends of the earth and say, Surely our fathers have inherited lies, worthlessness and unprofitable things. Will a man make gods for himself, which are not gods?" Jeremiah (Yirmeyahu) 16:19-20 NKJV.

I discovered that I had inherited lies and false doctrines from the fathers of my faith. I discovered that the faith which I had been steeped in had made gods which were not gods, and I saw very clearly how many could say "Lord, Lord" and not really know the Messiah or do the will of the Father, because they had actually rejected His commandments. I discovered that many of these lies were not just minor discrepancies but critical errors which could possibly have the effect of keeping me out of the New Jerusalem if I continued to practice them. (Revelation 21:27; 22:15).

While part of the problem stemmed from false doctrines which have crept into the Christian religion, it also had to do with anti-Semitism imbedded throughout the centuries which intentionally stripped the Christian religion of anything perceived as "Jewish." I even discovered translation errors in the very Scriptures that I was basing my beliefs upon. A good example is the next verse from the Prophet Jeremiah (Yirmeyahu) where most translations read: *"Therefore behold, I will this once cause them to know, I will cause them to know My hand and My might; and they shall know that My Name is the LORD."* Jeremiah (Yirmeyahu) 16:21 NKJV.

Could our Heavenly Father really be telling us that His Name is "the LORD?" This is a title, not a name and by the way, won't many people be crying out "Lord, Lord"

and be told that He never knew them? It is obvious that you should know someone's name in order to have a relationship with them. How could you possibly say that you know someone if you do not even know their name? So then we must ask: "What is the Name of our Heavenly Father?" The answer to this seeming mystery lies just beneath the surface of the translated text. In fact, if most people took the time to read the translators notes in the front of their Bible they would easily discover the problem.

You see the Name of our Creator is found in the Scriptures almost 7,000 times, although long ago a false doctrine was perpetrated regarding speaking the Name. It was determined that the Name either could not, or should not, be pronounced, and therefore it was replaced. Thus, over the centuries the Name of the Creator which was given to us so that we could know Him and be, not only His children, but also His friends, (Isaiah 41:8, James 2:23, John 15:15) was suppressed and altered. You will now find people using descriptions, titles and variations to replace the Name such as: God, Lord, Adonai, Jehovah and Ha Shem ("The Name") in place of the actual Name which was declared in Scriptures. What a tragedy and what a mistake!

One of the Ten Commandments, also known as the Ten Words, specifically instructs us not to take the Name of the Creator "in vain" and *"He will not hold him guiltless who takes His Name in vain."* (Exodus 20:7). Most Christians have been taught that this simply warns of using the Name lightly or in the context of swearing or in some other disrespectful manner. This certainly is one aspect of the commandment, but if we look further into

the Hebrew word for vain - שׁוא (pronounced shaw) we find that it has a deeper meaning in the sense of "desolating, uselessness, emptiness, nothingness or naught."

Therefore, we have been warned not only to avoid using the Name lightly or disrespectfully, but also not to bring it to naught, which is exactly what has been done over the centuries. The Name of our Creator which we have the privilege of calling on and praising has been suppressed to the point where most Believers do not even know the Name, let alone use it.

This sounds like a conspiracy of cosmic proportions and it is. Anyone who believes in the Scriptures must understand that there is a battle between good and evil. There is a Prince of Darkness, Satan, who understands very well the battle which has been raging since the creation of time. He will do anything to distract or destroy those searching for the truth, and he is very good at what he does. He is the Master of Deception and the Father of Lies, and he does not want the truth to be revealed. His goal is to steal, kill and destroy. (John 10:10). The enemy has operated both openly and behind the scenes over the centuries to infect, deceive, distract and destroy Believers with false doctrine. He truly is a wolf in sheep's clothing, and his desire is to rob the Believer of blessings and life.

As you read this book I hope that you will see how he has worked his deception regarding "Names." We are given wonderful promises in the Scriptures concerning blessings for those who obey the commandments. Sadly, many Believers have been robbed of those blessings due to

false doctrines which teach them to not keep the commandments, thus turning them into lawless individuals. Their belief is not followed by righteous works thereby making their faith empty and, to some extent, powerless.

My hope is that every reader has an eye opening experience and is forever changed. I sincerely believe that the truths which are contained in this book and the entire "Walk in the Light" series are essential to avoid the great deception which is being perpetrated upon those who profess to believe in, and follow the Holy One of Yisra'el.

This book, and the entire series, is intended for anyone who is searching for the truth. Depending upon your particular religion, customs and traditions, you may find some of the information to be contrary to the doctrines and teachings which you have read or heard throughout your life. Please realize, however, that none of the information is meant to criticize anyone or any faith, but merely to reveal truth.

The information contained in this book should stir up some things or else there would be no reason to have written it in the first place. The ultimate question is whether the contents align with the Scriptures and the will of the Creator. My goal is to strip away the layers of tradition which many of us have inherited and get to the core of the faith which is described in the Scriptures commonly called "The Bible."

This book should challenge your thinking and your beliefs and hopefully aid you on your search for truth. My prayer for you is that of the Apostle Paul, properly known as Shaul, in his letter to the Ephesian assembly that: "*17. . . the Father of esteem, would give you a spirit of wisdom and*

revelation in the knowledge of Him,[18] the eyes of your understanding being enlightened so that you know what is the expectation of His calling, and what are the riches of the esteem of His inheritance in the set-apart ones,[19] and what is the exceeding greatness of His power toward us who are believing, according to the working of His mighty strength." Ephesians 1:17-19 The Scriptures.

I

In the Beginning

This book, as the title indicates, is about names and their meaning: a subject which is not given much thought in America these days, but throughout history and in other areas of the world it is extremely significant. Quite often in my travels someone will ask me the origin or meaning of my name. For years I would simply indicate that I did not know without giving much reflection to the question. In my country we are generally more concerned with how a name sounds rather than what it means. I later found out through my studies that Hebrew names have a very specific and important meaning in life and throughout the Scriptures. According to Proverbs 22:1: "*A good name is to be chosen rather than great riches.*" Ecclesiastes 7:1 declares: "*A good name is better than precious ointment.*"

In fact, while studying the "Old Testament"[1] I discovered that it was generally imperative to learn the origin of a person's name in the Hebrew language in order to understand their significance. I also found out that some very important names had been hidden from me, names which I needed to know.

The Hebrew word for "name" is shem (שֵׁם) although shem has a deeper meaning and is also defined as "a mark or memorial of individuality" and implies "honor, authority, character and renown." We see other words in Hebrew which contain shem within them such as "wind" or "breath" - n'shemah (נְשָׁמָה) and "skies or heavens" – shamayim (שָׁמַיִם). We also read that the word for "hear" – shema (שָׁמַע) contains shem. The relationship between "hear" and "name" seems to indicate that a name should be spoken and thus heard. When words are spoken they are invisible to the eye, but they can be heard like the wind. Sounds can be very powerful, they can evoke joy or instill fear. Therefore, from all of these words which share the same root we can gather the deeper meaning of the word "name" (shem) which is not just an identifier or a label, but rather it is the very essence and character of an individual: both seen and unseen.

With that understanding we can begin our review of names in the Scriptures. Our discussion starts from the beginning because it was during the creation process that language developed. The Scriptures record that things were given descriptions as they were created. For instance light was called "day" and darkness was called "night" and the expanse of the sky was called "shamayim" (שָׁמַיִם). (Beresheet (Genesis) 1:5, 1:8)[2].

While many aspects of creation were provided words to describe them, the first time we read of anything having an actual name in the Scriptures are the four rivers that flowed out of a garden named Eden: 1) the Pishon, 2) the Gihon, 3) the Hideqel and 4) the Euphrates, although

we are not told when the garden or these rivers were actually named. We are told that male and female were called "Adam" (אדם) in the day they were created (Beresheet 5:2). The word "adam" can refer to an individual human being or the species of mankind.

After being created, "Adam" was placed in the Garden to work it and to guard it. The male Adam then gave names to every living creature (Beresheet 2:19-20). He also gave the title "woman" to his helper  and counterpart (Beresheet 2:20) and later named her Hawah (חוה) (Beresheet 3:20). He named her Hawah because "she became the mother of all living" and that is what Hawah means in Hebrew – "life giver." Her name described her purpose and her essence.

Now notice right here that we have a problem because anyone who attended Sunday School has learned that the wife of Adam was named Eve - Right? Sadly, that is simply not true, and all you have to do is read the Hebrew Scriptures to easily discern her real name. Since most people in the world cannot read Hebrew, they must rely upon flawed translations which contain numerous errors, especially when it comes to the treatment of names. I know that this may be a blow to those who hold to the inerrancy of their favorite translation but the simple fact is that most modern English translations of the Scriptures contain errors – some are minor while others may be considered critical.[3]

Throughout this book we will look at various names that have been altered, suppressed and replaced.

This process of discovery will hopefully lead you on the path of restoration so that you can accurately read and understand things which have been hidden within the pages of Scripture. Ultimately, you will be able to answer the question posed in the following Proverb:

"*Who has ascended into heaven, or descended?*
Who has gathered the wind in His fists?
Who has bound the waters in a garment?
Who has established all the ends of the earth?
What is His Name, and what is His Son's Name,
if you know?"

Proverbs (Mishle) 30:4

This Proverb, called Mishle (מִשְׁלֵי) in Hebrew, has long been considered to be a riddle by many "Jewish"[4] sages. The Mishle is clearly referring to the Creator of the universe and His Son. It implicitly infers that they both have Names which can be known. The reason why this issue has been a riddle to the sages is because they typically have not recognized the Son of God nor do they know His Name. At the same time, while they no doubt know the Name of the Father, they rarely, if ever, use the Name.

Christians, on the other hand, believe in the Son of God and they call Him "Jesus," although that name is not accurate according to the Scriptures and provable history, nor is it the Name which the Mishle is seeking. Also, while Christians claim to know the Name of the Son, very few know or use the Name of the Father.

Therefore, it seems that this Mishle is indeed a mystery worthy of further investigation, and one of the primary goals of this book will be to reveal the answer which could quite possibly change your life.

2

Lost in Translation

While every human being on the planet has a name, we often overlook the significance of names. This may have resulted because the naming process has become so common that even animals are given names. I must admit that not only do my child's pet dogs and cats have names, but also her ducks, chickens and stuffed animals. Despite the fact that names have become common, they are essential to human civilization, and without them we would be unable to properly identify, communicate and relate to one another.

Our Creator placed within each of us a certain desire to hear our name and know another's name. People generally enjoy hearing their names spoken, and a nerve is usually struck within us when someone calls us by the wrong name - especially when the person is expected to know our name. This has happened to me so many times, I lost count years ago. For some reason, people often call me Scott - not Joe, Bob or Ralph, always Scott.

Maybe my parents messed up and gave me the wrong name at birth. I may never know the reason why, but all through my life this would happen and when I was

younger it would really bother me. As I grew older I became accustomed to it, although I must confess, when someone that I have known for many years calls me Scott, it still makes me uncomfortable about our relationship. After all, if they cannot even get my name right, how well do they really know me, and even more importantly, how much do they care about knowing me!

There is something powerful about remembering and using a person's name. It is soothing to the other person to hear their name spoken and it creates a connection between individuals. When you use another person's name, you make them feel special. This is why business men and women are trained to remember names. When I was in high school I received a scholarship to attend the Dale Carnegie Course in Human Relations and Public Speaking. The first thing that we were taught was to memorize the names of everyone else that was taking the course. This is how strongly the people at the Dale Carnegie Institute feel about names and I agree with their emphasis on this issue.

All you need to do is observe expectant parents a few months before the birth of their child to appreciate the importance of a name. You will probably witness them pouring over books of baby names and most likely they will have a list of possibilities, depending upon their child's gender. Their desire is to select the perfect name for their little one and this process seems to confirm that there is something embedded within us by our Creator which makes our names so important.

Throughout this book we will be looking at, not only the Names of the Father and the Son, but also names of people who lived thousands of years ago. Originally,

their names were written and spoken in Hebrew. In order to understand the correct meaning and pronunciation of these names they need to be viewed in their original language. One thing that needs to be made very clear at this point is the fact that names must be transliterated - not translated. Translation tells us what a name means but unless it is in the original Hebrew, it does not necessarily tell us how the name is pronounced. Transliteration is the process whereby the name is spelled in such a way that a person is able to pronounce the name properly. A name may have a particular meaning or description but you always refer to the person by their name, not the meaning of their name.

Using our example of Hawah we can see that her name was spelled חוה in the Hebrew language and transliterated using the letters h a w a h in the English language. The first letter in the name is het (ח) and has a throaty "h" sound. The second letter is a vav (ו) and although modern Hebrew gives this letter a "v" sound it is generally believed that it had a "w" sound in ancient Hebrew. The final letter is hay (ה) and has an "h" sound.

If we were in her presence and wanted to speak with her we would not address her by saying "Hi, Life giver" or "Hello, mother of all living beings." Instead, we would simply call her by her name which is pronounced: Hawah. Also, you might speak another language where "Eve" actually means "life giver" but you would still not refer to her as Eve, because her name is Hawah. She may not understand your particular translation of her name and she certainly would not consider your translation to be her name.

In the transliteration process, we always try to keep the original sound, so that while spellings change from language to language, the name is always pronounced the same. In this way two things are preserved: 1) The proper pronunciation in the original tongue, and 2) The proper meaning in the original language.

Let me give a simple example. My name is Todd in English. It is also Todd in Chinese, Japanese, Russian, Italian, French, Hebrew as well as every other language on the face of the earth. While each language will use their own symbols or characters to spell my name, it should still sound the same, albeit there will obviously be some deviations due to accents and other linguistic factors. Further, while my name might mean: "one heck of a handsome, intelligent and down right swell guy" in some foreign dialect you would not address me by the translation of my name - even if I did enjoy hearing it. Instead, you would simply use my name: Todd.

No matter where I go on this planet, I introduce myself as Todd, and I expect to be called Todd. When I arrive in a new country I do not go to the local library, search out what my name means in that dialect, if anything at all, and then call myself by that new definition or phrase. That would be ridiculous. It is just as ridiculous to change names of people in the Scriptures simply because the text has been translated into a different language.

This may seem to be common sense but there are those who argue that pronunciation is meaningless and the most important thing is that the meaning of the name is translated. I am arguing that both are important, and as we continue, it should become obvious why this is the case.

3

The Name of God?

Having discussed the significance of names to mankind and recognizing that this appears to be something that the Creator placed within each one of us, would it not stand to reason that He also has a Name? Christians and Jews alike often talk of God and their belief in the same God. They use the term God as if it were actually the Name of the Almighty. While many use the word "God" when referring to the Creator of the universe as described in the Sefer Beresheet (Book of Genesis), the word "god" is and can be used to refer to any deity, whether Christian, Jewish, Muslim, Hindu or otherwise.

Different religions may have different ways of writing the word in English: Christians use GOD, Jews use G-D or G-d, and others use God or god. They all sound the same, and the only way you can tell the difference is when they are written. So, in essence, I could sit in a room with a Hindu and say: "I love GOD" and the Hindu could respond: "I love God too." In reality we would be referring to completely different entities, but from our statements it would appear that we are both on the same page in our beliefs and ideologies. This is because we are using a

generic descriptor and not a name. As a result, the stage is being set for potential disaster when we use the same title for the Creator of the universe described in the Scriptures as heathens[5] use to call their deity. If you are ecumenical then this is probably just fine, but if you are a Believer interested in promoting the truth, then I suggest you make certain that you are speaking the truth.

Let us take a look at some common definitions for the word "god" found in popular dictionaries: "a being conceived as the perfect, omnipotent, omniscient originator and ruler of the universe, the principal object of faith in monotheistic religions" or "a being of supernatural powers or attributes, believed in and worshipped by a people" or "an image of a supernatural being, an idol."[6] The word god is also defined as: "any of various beings conceived of as supernatural and immortal" or "a person or thing being deified."[7] According to these definitions, it seems that the term lacks specificity and could be used to describe any one of the thousands of deities or beings which are worshipped around the world.

Now let us look a little further at this seemingly generic word. The Encyclopedia Britannica, 11th edition, states "GOD – the common Teutonic word for a personal object of religious worship . . . applied to all those superhuman beings of the heathen mythologies. The word 'god' on the conversion of the Teutonic races to Christianity was adopted as the name of the one Supreme Being . . ." Teutonic, of course, refers to those of Germanic origin who were generally steeped in polytheistic beliefs contrary to the faith presented in the Scriptures. One of their Chief gods was Odin, also known

as Wodin where the word Wednesday comes from. The fourth day of the week, as with all of the other days in the modern calendar, was named after a pagan god. In this case - Wodin's Day.

According to the Webster's Twentieth Century Dictionary, Unabridged 1st Edition: "The word [God] is common in Teutonic tongues . . . It was applied to heathen deities and later, when the Teutonic peoples were converted to Christianity, the word was elevated to the Christian sense." The word "god" was used by heathens to describe their pagan deities and was later applied to the Creator of the universe when the Teutonic people converted to Christianity. In other words, they brought some of their pagan concepts with them when they became Christians.

This, we shall see, is quite common and occurred regularly throughout history. Sometimes it was done inadvertently, out of ignorance, while at other times it was done intentionally and systematically in the process known as syncretism[8] which is the merging together of two religions. In either case, the fact that it happened does not make it right, and true restoration involves ridding our belief system of inherited pagan influences. The Scriptures provide us with more of a reason to be cautious concerning the word "god."

The Prophet Isaiah, whose proper Hebrew name is Yeshayahu (ישעיהו), gave a warning to an apostate people in the end-times, and a typical English translation reads as

follows: "*But you are those who forsake the LORD, who forget my holy mountain, who prepare a table before Gad, and who fill a drink offering for Meni.*" Yeshayahu 65:11. In case you did not know, both Gad and Meni are pagan deities.

"Gad is usually interpreted as the well-known Syrian or Cannanite deity of 'Good Luck' or 'Fortune', and Meni the deity of 'Destiny'. This Gad is written in the Hebrew as GD (גד), but the Massoretes afterwards vowel-

pointed it, adding an "a" to give us "Gad." However we find other references in Scriptures to a similar deity, if not the same one, also spelt GD (גד) in the Hebrew text but this time vowel pointed to read "Gawd" or "God" (Joshua 11:17, 12:7, 13:5), where we find "Baal-Gawd" or "Baal-God," according to the vowel-pointed Massoretic Hebrew text. This

Baal-Gawd or Baal-God was obviously a place named after their deity."[9]

The location is given in the Scriptures as "*in the Valley of Lebanon below Mount Hermon*" (Joshua 11:17) also known as Ceasarea Philippi, Banias and Panias. This city was steeped in pagan religious beliefs and practices and even to this day you can find the remains of numerous temples couched along side one another in the religious district of the community.

According to the Keil & Delitzsch commentaries: "There can be no doubt . . . that Gad, the god of good fortune . . . is the deified planet Jupiter. This star is called by the Arabs "the greater luck" as being the star of good fortune; and . . . if Gad is Jupiter, nothing is more

probable than that Meni is Venus; for the planet Venus is also regarded as a star of prosperity, and is called by the Arabs "the lesser luck."[10]

Since the name of Baal-God, has roots which are found throughout pagan cultures, it is my opinion that his name should never be attributed to the Creator of the universe.[11] The word "God" is not the Name of the Creator, and the use of the words GOD, God, G-D or G-d to describe the Creator of the universe found in the Scriptures is not appropriate. I believe it is a disservice to the Almighty. Altering the name or title of a false deity by capitalizing all of the letters or putting a hyphen in the middle does not change the fact that it is the name of a false diety.

Using the previous example of my name – If some one calls me Scott or SCOTT, they still got my name wrong, and it does not make me feel any better whether they capitalize the letters or modify the spelling. Imagine how the Almighty feels when His people use the name or title of a false deity when referring to Him.[12]

The problem with the use of this title can be demonstrated by reviewing the Masonic philosophy. Masonry is, in essence, a religion which is expressed in symbols. One of the most important symbols in Masonry is the square and compass with the letter "G" in the middle. Early initiates are told that the "G" stands for God which makes Masonry palatable for many Christian members who do not delve any deeper. As one progresses through the many levels of Masonry, they will be told that the "G" has different meanings, until they ultimately come to understand it as the "generative principle" or the male reproductive organ. The phallus as we see in the largest Masonic monument in America, is none other than an obelisk which is  simply sun god worship in its most ancient form.

Interestingly, on the aluminum cap of this immense phallic symbol, known as the Washington monument, one will find inscribed the words "Laus Deo" which means "Praise be to Deo." Some translate "Deo" to mean "God" but it was originally the name of a pagan fertility goddess, Demeter, who was allegedly the mother of Dionysus, a pagan savior. The God or "G" that is being exalted through these symbols is none other than the sun god, Osiris. Thus in this one organization the word "God" has many different meanings depending upon a person's level of understanding, and at its' very core is sun god worship.

It is my hope that through this one simple example, the reader can plainly see the dangers of using titles such as "God." The Hebrew word used to describe the Almighty in the Scriptures is Elohim (אלהים). Elohim is plural and accurately identifies the Creator of the universe Who said: "Let _Us_ make man in _Our_ image." Beresheet 1:26. While the Elohim of the Scriptures reveals Himself in different ways, at the same time He is One[13] and His Name is One. (Zekaryah 14:9).[14] When we look at the Hebrew Scriptures we find the word Elohim whenever the text references what is generally termed God in an English

"Bible."[15]

Therefore, if you want to refer to the Creator of the universe, the proper Scriptural description is Elohim. From this point onward I will use the word Elohim instead of God. I will also replace it in any references which I cite from outside sources for the sake of accuracy and consistency.

4

The Lord

As with the word God, I hear many Christians and Jews calling upon the name of "The LORD," magnifying the name, praising the name and exalting the name. They refer to the Name but they rarely ever use the Name of the  Almighty. In fact, most people do not even know the Name of "The LORD" so instead they use the non-specific title "LORD." This is interesting since most other religions in the world have names for their gods or deities, such as Brahma, Vishnu and Shiva (the Hindu Trinity), Buddha and Allah. There are literally hundreds, if not thousands, of deities throughout the world, all with names which can be known and spoken.

Despite this indisputable reality, Catholics, Protestants and Jews have chosen to use the non-exclusive title of God or "Lord" for their deity instead of a name. This is simply a tradition which I believe has resulted in a disservice to the Almighty as well as to those who desire to know and serve Him.

The word "lord" has been defined in the

Westminster Desk Dictionary of the English Language as follows: "1. a person who has dominion over others, as a feudal superior. 2. a person who is a leader in a profession. 3. a titled nobleman or peer, as in Great Britain. 4. Lords. See House of Lords. 5. (cap) God or Jehovah. 6. (cap) the Savior, Jesus Christ. – v.t. 7. lord it over, to domineer over."

As can be seen, the word has primarily been applied to men. The title "Lord" also comes from paganism and is linked to Baal worship. It is interesting to note that Baal (בעל) in Hebrew actually means "lord."

> Baal (Hb ba'al, "lord" in the sense of owner or master, e.g., of a wife, a slave, a piece of property.) Most commonly it is a divine appellative (not a personal name) and as such appears as a component in many personal and local names.
> The character of the Baal cult has been much illuminated by the discovery of the Canaanite mythological tablets of Ugarit*. The title Baal, "lord," was applied to several gods; but when used without further qualification it signified the storm-god Hadad* (Akkadian Adad or Addu). In the Ugaritic texts he has the title Aliyan, "he who prevails" (Albright). As the storm-god who rules the weather he is the giver of fertility.
> 16

In the Scriptures, whenever you read about the Gentiles worshipping Baal, they are worshipping a deity whose name literally means "Lord." Further, this title has been linked to the Etruscan deity Larth, the Teutonic deity of war, Loride, as well as to Lordo, a demon. Sadly, this is exactly the same title that most Jews and Christians

currently use to refer to Elohim. It may not be spelled with all capital letters like the translators spelled it in replacing the Name of the Almighty with "LORD," but it sure does sound the same.

The titles "LORD" and "Lord" sound the same because they are, in fact, identical. The words and sounds of our mouths are important, and it would seem reasonable that through our speech we should try to avoid any semblance of Baal worship or the worship of any other god for that matter. Read the following Scripture passage and decide for yourself whether or not it applies directly to what we see today in the religious systems that claim to serve the Almighty: *"For I will take from her mouth the names of the Baals, and they shall be remembered by their name no more."* Hosea 2:16-17 NKJV.

"Baal is a generic term for god in many of the Syro-Arabian languages. As the idolatrous nations of that race had several gods, this word, by means of some accessory distinction, became applicable as a name to many different deities. See Baal-Berith, See Baal-peor; See Baal-Zebub. There is no evidence, however, that the [Yisra'elites] ever called [The Almighty] by the name of Baal; for the passage in Hosea 2:16, which has been cited as such, only contains the word baal as the sterner, less affectionate representative of husband. It is spoken of the master and owner of a house (Exodus 22:7; Judges 19:22); of a landholder (Job 31:39); of an owner of cattle (Exodus 21:28; Isaiah 1:3); of a lender of money, i.e. creditor (Deuteronomy 15:2); also of the head of a family (Leviticus

21:4); and even of the Assyrians (or the princes) as conquerors of nations (Isaiah 16:8)."[17] As we can see, Baal, which means Lord, was never used by the Israelites (Yisra'elites)[18] to refer to the Name of Elohim. The usage today is the result of bad traditions and the translations which promote them.

Look at how blatantly incorrect certain English translations are when they replace the Name of Elohim with a title. *"He turns the shadow of death into morning and makes the day dark as night; He calls for the waters of the sea and pours them out on the face of the earth; The LORD is His Name."* Amos 5:8 NKJV. "The LORD" is obviously *not* His Name and by tampering with the text, the translators have destroyed the very purpose of this passage – to declare the Name.

Read another passage in Amos which again, demonstrates the error. *"He who builds His layers in the sky, and has founded His strata in the earth; Who calls for the waters of the sea, and pours them out on the face of the earth - The LORD is His Name."* Amos 9:6 NKJV. Again, "The LORD" is a title, not a name and the translation error is quite obvious.

Now look at the warning provided by the Prophet Jeremiah (Yirmeyahu)[19] concerning the relation between Baal worship and forgetting the Name of The Creator. *"[25] I have heard what the prophets say who prophesy lies in My Name. They say, 'I had a dream! I had a dream!' [26] How long will this continue in the hearts of these lying prophets, who prophesy the delusions of their own minds? [27] <u>They think the dreams they tell one another will make my people forget My Name, just as their fathers forgot My Name through Baal</u>*

worship." Yirmeyahu 23:25-27. This is similar to what has occurred over the recent centuries. Just as ancient Yisra'el forgot the Name, so too have many Jewish and Christian Believers forgotten the Name of the Almighty because of the use of Baal or rather: "The LORD."

On any given Sabbath in almost every Jewish synagogue[20] you will hear "G-D," "The LORD" and "HaShem" being praised, while on any given Sunday morning in almost any Christian "church"[21] building you will undoubtedly hear the following utterances resonating throughout the worship service: "Praise the LORD" and "Glory to God."

While these well-meaning worshippers may desire to worship the Elohim of Yisra'el with their hearts, they are not doing so with their lips. Instead they may be inadvertently offering up worship to Baal. Rarely do they ever mention the Name of the True Elohim except perchance when they sing "HalleluYah," which is a Hebrew word that offers praise to the Name of the Creator, not to "The LORD" as many are taught. So then, the Name is sometimes praised in worship services, although much of the time unknowingly.

I am sure that many would respond to my observation as follows: "Although these worshippers may not be saying the right words with their lips, it is their heart which is important." This is partially true, the heart is vital, but the point that I am trying to demonstrate is that partially correct worship is not what pleases the Almighty, He wants us to get it <u>all</u> right. Read the Book of Malachi and see how Elohim feels about improper worship.[22] Also refer to the Psalm of David which states:

"Let the words of my mouth <u>and</u> the meditation of my heart be acceptable in Your sight . . ." Psalms 19:14.

It is not just the heart, but also the utterances from our mouths that matter and we need to identify the Elohim that we worship with our lips as well as with our hearts. To illustrate this important point, imagine if a group of satan worshippers, muslims or hindus visited a local Christian worship service dressed in their "Sunday best." They could sing a majority of the hymns to their "god" and their "lord" and they would be worshipping with their hearts, right along side the Christian worshippers.

On the surface, this ecumenical gathering could appear to be in perfect unity. This is because of the use of the generic terms and titles being used by the worshippers. Rarely do you hear a specific name in Christian worship and when it is used, it is typically wrong. The words in much Christian worship have become so generic that many songs could be sung to most any "god." For instance, some popular songs in modern Christianity proclaim "Our God is an Awesome God" and "Great is the Lord" but they never specifically identify the god or lord by name so any religion could borrow these songs and sing these choruses about their gods.

An illustration of the use of titles and the diluting effect that it has had can be seen in the popular song by the former Beatle George Harrison entitled "My Sweet Lord." At first glance, this sounds like a wonderful song which could be sung by Christians. As the song progresses the singer declares: "My sweet lord . . . I really want to see you

". . . really want to be with you . . . I really want to know you . . . Really want to go with you . . . my sweet lord." When the chorus starts chanting "halleluyah" in the background it seems clear that this must be a Christian song which is being sung to "Jesus" but things take a drastic turn at the end of the song when the chorus alters their chant from "halleluyah" to "hare krishna, krishna krishna, hare hare" which is the Hare Krishna Maha-Mantra. According to Srila Prahapada: "Chanting the transcendental vibration . . . is the sublime method for reviving our transcendental consciousness or krishna consciousness."[23]

So there is no mistake which "lord" George Harrison is referring to, the chorus then recites a sacred Hindu prayer from the Guru Gita found within the Skanda Purana which praises the "trinity" of Brahma, Vishnu and Shiva as follows: "guror Brahma, guror Vishnuh, guror devo Maheshwarah, gurors sakshaat para Brahma tasmei shree gurave namah" which means "Guru is Brahma (the god of creation), Guru is Vishnu (the god of sustenance), Guru is the god Shiva (the god of annihilation) and Guru is verily the Supreme God. My salutations to that auspicious Guru."

This song which begins by apparently referring to one of the Christian trinity as "lord" ends up praising the Hindu Trinity, Brahma, Vishnu and Shiva as "lord." It is a not so subtle attempt by George Harrison to indoctrinate his listeners into eastern mysticism. The word "lord" is a non-offensive way of presenting his "lord" to Western

society which also uses the word "lord" to worship their "god."

This, of course, is exactly what the ecumenical and universal movements promote. In their attempt to unify all denominations and religions, they "water down" their doctrines so as not to offend anyone. They want everyone to be able to hold hands and sing "Kumbaya my lord, Kumbaya" regardless of their individual religious affiliation. Interestingly, this may not be such a bad idea if my research is correct. According to my investigation Kumbaya, also spelled "KumbaYah," originates from a song in the Angola-Nigeria region of Africa which is an invitation to the Almighty to "come by" and it refers to Elohim by His Hebrew Name. On second thought, maybe Christians should start singing KumbaYah in their worship services. At least it identifies the Name of the Creator and invites His presence.

There is a prayer in Christianity commonly referred to as "The LORD's Prayer" which goes as follows: "*9 Our Father in heaven, Hallowed be Your Name. 10 Your kingdom come. Your will be done on earth as it is in heaven. 11 Give us this day our daily bread. 12 And forgive us our debts, as we forgive our debtors. 13 And do not lead us into temptation, but deliver us from the evil one. For Yours is the kingdom and the power and the glory forever. Amen.*" Matthew (Mattithyahu) 6:9-13 NKJV. According to this prayer, we have a Father in Heaven and His Name is "hallowed." People pray this prayer and use the word "hallowed" on a daily basis although it is not a word typically used in society in any other context. The first question that anyone should ask is: What does it mean?

The Greek word for hallowed is hagiazo (αγιαζω) which means to make holy, i.e. (ceremonially) purify or consecrate; (mentally) to venerate. The Hebrew word used in this context is kadosh (קדש) which means "set apart." Both of these words reflect the fact that the Name should be treated carefully and reverently. Neither word gives the sense that the Name should be suppressed. When dealing with the Name of the Father, traditions of men have taken over and the concept of "hallowing" the Name has resulted in "suppressing" the Name.

The problem is that our Heavenly Father never told us to avoid or suppress His Name. In fact, time and time again, He revealed His Name. He expects us to exalt and esteem His Name, so how can we do this if we never speak The Name?

There are many titles that we can use to refer to Elohim which translate the proper esteem due Him. Lord is such a common word and is used to this day to refer to men of nobility or other positions and in my opinion it is not adequate to refer to El Shaddai.[24] I prefer the title Master which is Adonai (אדני) in Hebrew, because it more accurately reflects the relationship that is created when someone willingly becomes a bondservant[25] of the Almighty, although I try to avoid the use of titles whenever possible.

Anyone can observe from modern Christian worship that Christianity has truly forgotten the Name of the Creator, just as Yisra'el forgot the Name. The continued use of titles, especially that of Lord (Baal) only perpetuates the problem. I find this amazing because I spent most of my life in "church" hearing about the

mistakes that Yisra'el made and I was always astonished how they continually fell back into the worship of idols. The somewhat sympathetic, mostly patronizing tone used while referring to Yisra'el in that context carried with it a resounding assumption that Christianity was somehow immune from making those same mistakes.

The prevailing thinking was that while an individual Believer may fall prey to the wiles of the Devil,  the "System" of Christianity was certainly not subject to such deception, especially after the centuries of reforms initiated by Martin Luther and his contemporaries when Protestants supposedly shook off the errors perpetrated by the Roman Catholic Church. I grew up believing that "Church" doctrine was pure and it was the individual that needed saving and cleansing. I was wrong!

I now plainly see that the "System" has been corrupted for centuries – but why should anyone expect any different. We can easily read in the Scriptures how, time after time, Yisra'el was tarnished and besmirched through disobedience and rebellion while Elohim actually visibly appeared and dwelled in their midst. That being the case, why should Christianity be any different than ancient Yisra'el. Even a cursory review of the Christian religion shows that it has been plagued with corruption almost from its inception.[26] So then, like Yisra'el, the Christian religion is not immune from idolatry or false doctrines. This statement is equally applicable to modern Rabbinic Judaism.[27]

If Christians and Jews profess to serve Elohim as

did ancient Yisra'el, then they will undoubtedly be subjected to the same struggles, deceptions and failures. Like ancient Yisra'el, Christianity and Judaism have both failed to maintain the truth and now restoration through the Messiah is required to set things straight. One of the things currently being revealed and restored is the Name of the Father.

5

The Name of the Father

The Scriptures are full of examples of the importance and meaning of names. The Book in the Torah,[28] which most English translations call Exodus is actually called Shemot (שמות) in Hebrew and means "Names." So then, the major theme of this Book is not the Exodus from Egypt (Mitsrayim)[29] but rather "Names," which is exactly how the Book begins: *"These are the names of the sons of Yisra'el . . ."* Shemot 1:1.

The Prophet Yeshayahu proclaimed that Elohim divided the waters before Yisra'el *"to make for Himself an everlasting Name."* Yeshayahu 63:12. With that understanding, you end up reading the text with an entirely different focus and see that the Exodus from Mitsrayim was primarily about the Name of Elohim, not simply the names of the children of Yisra'el who were freed from bondage.

Throughout the entire "Old Testament" which is better known as the Tanakh[30] we see that all of the Prophets had names with meanings which were

significant to their ministries. At times they would even name their children with prophetically significant names. (see Hoshea 1).[31] The Almighty has a Name and it is not "God," nor is it "The LORD." In fact, the Name of our Creator is found 6,823 times in the Canonized Scriptures,[32] but many do not know it and therefore are unable to answer the riddle posed in the Sefer Mishle[33] – *"What is His Name, and what is His Son's Name, if you know?"*

Currently, the Name of Elohim has been suppressed or forgotten by much of the world. The reason for this is largely the result of a false doctrine propagated by ancient Pharisaic Judaism, and adopted by Christianity, which teaches that the Name is ineffable or unspeakable and therefore it must be avoided, hidden or altered. As a result, the Yisra'elites stopped using the Name, except for the High Priest who would speak it once a year during Yom Kippur – The Day of Atonement.

While the Name could still be read in the Hebrew Scriptures, it was not spoken. Rather the titles Adonai or Elohim were used as subtitles when the Scriptures were read. The Septuagint, which was the Greek translation of the Tanakh, replaced the Name with Kurios and the Latin Vulgate used Dominius. English translators continued this tradition and actually replaced the Name of the Almighty with the title: "The LORD." In some instances they also replaced the Name with "GOD" because their translations would otherwise sound absurd. Yehezqel 37:3 reads "יהוה אדני" which would be translated "O Lord the LORD" if they were consistent in their mistranslation, but they instead translated it as "O Lord GOD".

In order to show that they are replacing the Name,

the translators used all capital letters to signify the Name. Regrettably, it still sounds the same as the title of an English nobleman or pagan deity and what seems like such a pious and respectful act involves an alteration and a grievous mistranslation of the Scriptures. This apparently noble endeavor to protect the Name of the Almighty is quite possibly one of the greatest and most destructive deceptions perpetrated upon mankind. To this day you will find people continuing to replace the Name with Hebrew titles such as "HaShem" and "Adonai." While these may sound more accurate, because they are Hebrew, they are still incorrect when used to replace the Name of the Almighty.

"HaShem" (הֹשֵם) is a Hebrew word which means "The Name." Many orthodox Jews and Messianic Believers continue the same replacement error, but instead of using "GOD" or "LORD," they use "HaShem." The problem remains the same, they are replacing the Name, only in this case it is not even with a true title. Instead of referring to the Almighty by His Name they call Him "The Name." This is an awfully cold and impersonal reference to a loving Creator and I am very much opposed to this practice.

"Adonai" (אדני) is a Hebrew word meaning "master" which was often inserted into the Massoretic text by the Massoretes. The Massoretes were responsible for preserving the Tanakh but they were also renowned for their attempts to hide the true Name. Their motivation was apparently to prevent people from blaspheming the Name although some things are better left to the Almighty because ultimately they ended up altering the Scriptures.

They replaced the Name of the Almighty with the title "Adonai." This is a transgression of the commandment which states: *"You shall not add to the word which I command you, nor take from it, that you may keep the commandments . . ."* Devarim 4:2.

The Greeks have a god named Adonis, who is the same deity as the Roman sun god Mithras, who is the same deity as the Babylonian sun god Tammuz. I see no reason to replace the Name of my Elohim with the title "Adonai" when that is not His Name, especially when there is such similarity with the name of a pagan god. If you want to refer to the  Creator as your Master then by all means use the word Adonai, but I would not recommend replacing His Name with any title, including Adonai.

Ultimately, if Elohim did not want us to know and speak His Name, He would not have provided it to us nearly 7,000 times in the Scriptures, not counting all of the Non-Canonized Texts. Further, looking at the plain context of the Name as it is revealed in the Scriptures, it is clear that the Name was proclaimed (Devarim 32:3), spoken (Devarim 18:20), honored, worshipped and praised (Psalms 7:17, 69:30). The righteous long after the Name and remembrance of Elohim (Yeshayahu 26:8). The Levites were commanded to minister in the Name (Devarim 18:5), serve in the Name (Devarim 18:7) and bless in the Name (Devarim 21:5; see also Psalms 103:1). Yisra'el is called by the Name (Devarim 20:10). Boaz greeted in the Name (Ruth 2:4). King David blessed in the Name (1 Chronicles 16:2), he rejoiced in the Name (Psalms

20:5) and he called on the Name (Psalms 116). He sang out the honor of the Name (Psalms 66:2) and sang praises to the Name (Psalms 68:4). Solomon built a house for the Name (1 Kings 8:20; 2 Chronicles 2:4) and he was famous concerning the Name (1 Kings 10:1). Elijah called on the Name and fire came down from heaven (1 Kings 18:24). People would swear to tell the truth in the Name (2 Chronicles 18:15). There is majesty in the Name (Micah 5:4). The Name defends those who serve Him (Psalms 20:21). The righteous walk in the Name (Micah 4:5). The Name is a strong tower, the righteous run to it and are safe (Mishle 18:12). Our help is in the Name (Psalms 124:8) and we trust in the Name (Yeshayahu 50:10). We are to love the Name (Yeshayahu 56:6). The Name will be feared by the nations (Psalms 102:15) and declared in Tzion (Psalms 102:21). Whoever calls on the Name shall be saved (Joel 2:32; see also Romans 10:13). The Name endures forever (Psalms 72:17).

This is by no means an exhaustive list but I hope that it illustrates the fact that the Name of Elohim was used extensively throughout the ages and it is intended to be spoken in reverence.

The Name of the Almighty, The Elohim of Yisra'el, which appears nearly 7,000 times in the Scriptures is spelled 𐤉𐤄𐤅𐤄 in Ancient Hebrew Script and 𐤉𐤄𐤅𐤄 in the earliest known paleo-Hebrew pictograph script. The paleo-Hebrew pictographic script may reflect how the Name looked on the Tablets of the Ten Commandments which were written in stone by the Hand of Elohim or the first Torah Scroll written by Moses (Mosheh).[34] Ancient Hebrew, also known as paleo-

Hebrew, went through a variety of changes so it is not certain which script was used when Yisra'el left Mitsrayim but one thing is certain, the Name of Elohim was originally written and spoken in the Hebrew language.

There are numerous archaeological evidences which show the Name of YHWH in Ancient Hebrew Script. One of the most notable was the Moabite Stone, also known as the Mesha Stele, which is dated around 930 BC. Even when the Hebrew language was modernized some continued to spell the Name in Ancient Hebrew. Look at the following ancient manuscript of Tehellim 119:59-64 which is written in modern Hebrew except for the Name of the Creator which is written in Ancient Hebrew.

Seeing the Name of the Almighty in Hebrew script may seem awkward and unusual for many Christians who are accustomed to the Westernized, English King James Version of their Creator, but if you serve the Elohim described within the Scriptures you need to get used to the fact that He established the Hebrew language as a special language and He revealed His Name in Hebrew.

We know that modern Hebrew is not written the same as the original Hebrew language, but the letters in

modern Hebrew that correspond to the Ancient Hebrew letters are Yud (י) Hay (ה) Vav (ו) Hay (ה) or יהוה in Modern Hebrew and 𐤉𐤄𐤅𐤄 in Ancient Hebrew. It is important to understand that Hebrew is written from right to left so if you want to refer to the Tetragrammaton (the four letter Name of Elohim) using English letters you would spell it left to right, YHWH or YHVH. The letter depicted by the W and V is called Vav (v or w), but it is believed that in the ancient tongue it had a "w" sound.

Therefore, I prefer to spell the Name in English as YHWH although a literal consonant for consonant translation would be YHVH. There is speculation as to whether all four letters of the Name are consonants or vowels because each letter in the Name may also be pronounced as vowels in modern Hebrew. The four Hebrew letters א, ה, ו and י are sometimes called vowel letters.[35] This leads directly to the debate on how to pronounce the Name which is discussed in the following chapter.

6

Pronouncing the Name

The first question that typically comes to mind after discovering the true Name of YHWH is: How do we pronounce the Name? This is a highly debated subject and if you decide to research the matter for yourself you will no doubt find a variety of opinions along with people who vehemently defend and support their particular pronunciation. While the purpose of this book is not to convince you of any particular position, I feel that it is important to discuss the primary pronunciations.

The most traditional and popular pronunciation, by far, in Christianity is: Jehovah. The name Jehovah is often used to pronounce the Name of YHWH by translating the Tetragrammaton as JHVH and inserting the vowels from Adonai.

"This happened because Christian translators' ignorance of Hebrew failed to alert them that the 'vowel points' placed beneath the Name were to 'cue' the reader not to pronounce it, but to say Adonai instead. The man who gave us the hybrid word 'Jehovah' was Petrus Galatinus. You

can easily find that the letter "J" didn't even exist on the planet until about 1520 CE. The letter is less than 500 years old! "J" came from the letter YOD in Hebrew, and was brought into the Greek with the letter "IOTA," or our letter "I" since they had no "Y." Gradually, customs developed that put a tail on the letter I when it began a sentence, or was used as the first letter of a proper name. [36]

Both the Universal Jewish Encyclopedia and the Jewish Encyclopedia indicate that "Jehovah" is not a word at all. In fact, the name is a philological impossibility. So then, despite its' popularity, "Jehovah" cannot be the correct pronunciation of Name of the Almighty.

The most popular pronunciation of the Tetragrammaton in academia is Yahweh (Yah-way). There are volumes of research supporting this position and it is largely based upon philology and representations in ancient languages, such as Greek, which have rendered the Name as IAOYE. The historian Flavius Josephus wrote that the golden crown worn by the High Priest contained the Name of Elohim which "consists of four vowels." The Jewish War 5:5:7. Many interpret this passage to support the notion that the Tetragrammaton is four vowels which would result in a pronunciation sounding like: ee-ah-oo-ay. This is by no means the only possible pronunciation using Greek vowels since each vowel has different possible pronunciations.

It is important to recognize that while Josephus wrote The Jewish Wars in both Hebrew (or Aramaic) and

Greek, most of our English translations come from the Greek. The Greek language does not have consonants which equate to the Hebrew consonants contained in the Tetragrammaton and the Greeks translated all the letters in the Name YHWH as vowels. The Hebrew yud (י) became the Greek vowel iota (I), the Hebrew hay (ה) became the Greek vowel epsilon (E) and the Hebrew vav (ו) became the Greek vowel upsilon (Y). The Greeks considered all the letters in the Name of YHWH to be vowels thus the statement by Josephus, in the Greek language, that the letters on the crown of the High Priest were all vowels.

It appears that Josephus was explaining to a Greek speaking audience that the Name YHWH was spelled with all vowels because it was, in fact, spelled with all vowels in the Greek language. But just because the letters were considered vowels to the Greeks does not necessarily mean that they were vowels in the Hebrew language. In fact, the Hebrew letters yud (י), hay (ה) and vav (ו) only began to double as vowels in the 9th century B.C.E. Before that time they were exclusively used as consonants and even after the 9th century a yud (י) at the beginning of a word always constituted a consonant, never a vowel.37

This leads us to other possible pronunciations of the Name which view all of the Hebrew letters as consonants. We must begin our analysis by looking at the first two letters: yud (י) and hay (ה) which spell יה. They

are pronounced as Yah and there is not much dispute on this point. This was actually almost translated correctly once in the King James Version of the Bible. *"Sing unto God, sing praises to his name: extol him that rideth upon the heavens by his name JAH, and rejoice before him."* Psalms 68:4 KJV.

As was previously mentioned, there is no "J" in Hebrew so you would never pronounce the Name as "Jah." The poetic short form of YHWH is pronounced "Yah" and the New King James version actually corrected the error. Yah is also used in the Prophecy of Yeshayahu (Isaiah) 12:2, 24:6, 38:11 in the New King James Version. Sadly, these are the only instances where a reader gets a glimpse of the True Name of YHWH and most other modern English translations continue to replace the Name with the title "the LORD."

There are at least 47 other instances in the Tanakh where Yah (יה) is located in the Hebrew text but all of the modern English versions reflect the title "The LORD" instead of the Name. A point that warrants repeating is that when people say Hallelu<u>Yah</u> (הללויה) they are saying a Hebrew word which means "praise be to Yah." So while we can be quite certain that Yah is how we pronounce the beginning of the Name the ending pronunciation is where much debate exists.

The third Hebrew letter in the Name is vav (ו). While the vav (ו) now has a "v" sound in modern Hebrew, it is believed that it had a "w" sound in ancient Hebrew. As we shall see later in this discussion, many of our ancestors in the faith contained the Name of YHWH

within their names. You will notice in a preceding paragraph the correct Hebrew name of the Prophet called Isaiah is Yeshayahu. It is spelled ישעיהו in Hebrew, and it ends with the first three letters of the Name of YHWH. This is not the only name where this occurs and those three letters are usually always pronounced: "yahu" or "yahuw." The final Hebrew letter hay (ה) has an "h" sound. Therefore, many pronounce the Name as Ya-hu-wah.

I believe that a key to the correct pronunciation is found in the name commonly called "Judah." The first time that we see the name Judah in the Scriptures is when Leah conceives her fourth son: "*And she conceived again and bore a son, and said, 'Now I will praise YHWH.' Therefore she called his name Judah.*" Beresheet 29:35. The name Judah, properly pronounced Yahudah, stems directly from her statement "*Now I will praise YHWH.*" Many people interpret Yahudah to simply mean "praise," but as we can see, this is not correct.

The name which is commonly spelled and pronounced Judah in English is spelled 𐤉𐤄𐤅𐤃 in ancient Hebrew or יהודה in Modern Hebrew. Notice the similarity between יהודה (YHW<u>D</u>H) and יהוה (YHWH). The only difference is the dalet (ד) which has a "D" sound. If we take the dalet (ד) out of Yahudah we are left with YHWH, the Name of the Creator.

Therefore, if you believe that the Name of YHWH consists of all consonants then it would likely be pronounced Yahuwah rather than Yahweh. I believe that this will become even clearer when we look at the Name of

the Son in Chapter 9 as well as the names of certain prophets and patriarchs. It also seems consistent with the name of the first woman whose name meant "life giver." Remember that the name Ha<u>wah</u> (חוה) actually ends with the same two letters as YHWH (יהוה) so Yahu<u>wah</u> would be a consistent pronunciation.

There are many different people who believe in many different pronunciations. "John H. Skilton, *The Law and the Prophets*, pp. 223, 224, prefers 'Yahoweh'. The Assyrians transcribed the Name as 'Ya-u-a', so Mowinckle and other scholars prefer 'Yahowah'. Some scholars prefer 'Yehowah', because that is the way the Massoretes vowel-pointed it. (Whether this vowel pointing of the Name was done in truth, or whether it was done to 'disguise' the Name, in accordance with the instruction given in the Mishnaic text of *Tamid* vii.2 (= *Sota* vii.6), we do not know for certain. There is also the Rabbinical interpretation of the Massoretic text saying that the vowels e, o and a were added to the Name as a *Qere perpetuum* which means that the reading of Adonai or Elohim is to be used instead. However, there is no definite proof that the Massoretes originally did it for this reason)."[38]

In this period of restoration which the Assembly of Believers is currently experiencing, it is important to remain teachable. I have very good friends who have different opinions and I certainly do not consider the pronunciation to be a basis for contention since it is still the subject of debate and speculation. The point is that we are all trying to get it right.

There are some who believe, not that the Name is ineffable or unspeakable, but simply that we do not know

how to pronounce it, therefore, at this time we cannot utter the Name. My belief is that the Almighty appreciates our efforts, and our prayerful search to know Him, and His Name, is something which pleases Him. I can tell you that I have been blessed in my quest to discover and use the Name of the Almighty and I see no Scriptural precedent for not using the Name. I do not take this issue lightly and believe that if you perform a diligent search of the Scriptures you will ascertain that YHWH places great importance in His Name.

The point of this discussion is not to convince you that any particular pronunciation is correct, but rather to reveal that there is a Name for the Almighty which has been hidden from those who seek and serve Him. We each have the ability to develop a personal relationship with the Almighty which involves speaking to Him and using His Name. I suggest that you introduce yourself to Him and ask the same in return.

Since there is disagreement on how to pronounce the Name, I will not transliterate the Name of the Almighty but rather I will use the four Hebrew letters transliterated into English as YHWH when I refer to His Name. That way while you are reading, you can pronounce it the way that you are most comfortable.

7

The Name in the Scriptures

At this point in the discussion it may be helpful to take a look at some Scripture passages to see how the Name was revealed and used by our ancestors in the faith. The first time that mankind began calling on the Name of YHWH was after the birth of Enosh. "*25 And Adam knew his wife again, and she bore a son and named him Seth, 'For Elohim has appointed another seed for me instead of Abel, whom Cayin killed'. 26 And as for Seth, to him also a son was born; and he named him Enosh. Then men began to call on the Name of YHWH.*" Beresheet 4:25-26.

This does not necessarily mean that the Name of YHWH was not spoken before this time. It could be referring to the fact men had to call upon the Name due to their fallen condition and inability to dwell in the presence of YHWH.

The next time that we read about someone calling on the Name of YHWH is found in the account of Abram who was later known as Abraham or Avraham. "*6 Abram traveled through the land as far as the site of the great tree of Moreh at Shechem. At that time the Canaanites were in the land. 7 YHWH appeared to Abram and said, 'To your offspring I will*

give this land'. So he built an altar there to YHWH, Who had appeared to him. ⁸ From there he went on toward the hills east of Bethel and pitched his tent, with Bethel on the west and Ai on the east. There he built an altar to YHWH and called on the Name of YHWH." Beresheet 12:6-8.

The Scriptures record four specific events where Abraham *"called on the Name of YHWH"* (Beresheet 12:8; 13:4; 21:33; 26:25) although it is clear that he used the Name throughout his life. (Beresheet 15:2; 16:5; 18:3).

During the account of the life of Abraham we see that Sarah "called the Name" of YHWH (Beresheet 16:13), King Abimelech used the Name (Beresheet 20:4), Lot used the Name (Beresheet 19:18) and Abraham's servant (Eliezer) prayed to YHWH, worshipped YHWH and spoke the Name YHWH to others (Beresheet 24:12-56). Isaac (Yitshaq)[39] prayed to YHWH as did his wife Rebecca (Ribkah)[40] (Beresheet 25:21-23). Jacob (Ya'akov)[41] also used the Name of YHWH (Beresheet 28:16).

YHWH described Himself as El Shaddai to Abraham, which means "Elohim Almighty" (Beresheet 17:1). After YHWH spared the life of Yitshaq on Mount Moriah, Abraham called the place YHWH Yireh because *"on the mountain YHWH provides."* Beresheet 22:14. I find that to be an interesting statement because as you look through Scripture it was typically on this mountain where  significant encounters with YHWH took place and tradition states that it is this very mountain where the Temple Mount is located in Jerusalem (Yahrushalaim).

YHWH said that He has chosen Yahrushalayim as a place for His Name to dwell (2 Chronicles 6:6). Therefore, this specific geographical location was chosen for the Name.

After Yisra'el (formerly Ya'akov) and his family went to Mitsrayim it appears that his descendents forgot the Name of YHWH. Even toward the end of the life of Yisra'el it seems that his relationship with YHWH may have waned because the Scriptures record that when he was on his way to Mitsrayim he stopped at Beersheba *"and brought offerings to the Elohim of his father Yitshaq."* Beresheet 46:1. At that place Elohim spoke to Yisra'el in a dream, not in person, and said *"I am the El, Elohim of your father."* Notice that he did not bring offerings to YHWH *his* Elohim, and YHWH said He was the Elohim *of his father.* Now there is no doubt that YHWH was also the Elohim of Yisra'el but there may have been a diminished intimacy and by the time his descendents had been in Mitsrayim for 400 years (Beresheet 15:13) it looks as if much had been forgotten, including the Name of YHWH.

Most people know that Sefer Shemot picks up with the children of Yisra'el being enslaved in Mistrayim for an

 extended period. As already mentioned, while the English title "Exodus" relates the text with the departure from Mistrayim, the Hebrew title Shemot (שמות) means "Names." Thus it is within the text of Shemot where the full revelation of the Name of YHWH is given to Mosheh. It is also where we see the Name being revealed to the nations of the world.

Mosheh was spared from death as an infant and

raised by the very people who sought to kill him. He was most likely a very intelligent and well educated man having been adopted into Pharaoh's household. He later fled Mitsrayim and became a shepherd in the Land of Midian. A prince became a shepherd who was reluctant to speak to the Hebrews,  maybe because he lost all confidence in his ability to speak or lead people. Maybe he did not know the Hebrew language or was simply slow of speech or stuttered.

In any event it is interesting to observe the life of Mosheh because in him we see a man that was chosen by Elohim from birth and directed through much of his life by Elohim before he ever knew Elohim. Like Abraham, he was raised in a pagan society and surrounded by the worship of false gods. He needed an encounter with the True Elohim and that is exactly what he got at the burning bush. The Scriptures record that *"the Messenger of YHWH"* appeared to him in a flame of fire from the midst of a bush. When Mosheh turned aside to see why the bush did not burn He met Elohim.

There is so much that we can learn from this one meeting and you will not be able to see it if you do not read the original Hebrew text. Hidden within this passage we see the un-translated Aleph Taw (את) not less than 20 times. Aleph (א) is the first letter of the Hebrew alphabet and Taw (ת) is the last letter of the Hebrew alphabet. Whenever you see את in the Hebrew text, it is typically un-translated and is often considered to be a mystery by

the sages. While the grammatical function of the Aleph Taw (את) is to point to a direct definite object, it is often viewed as a hinted reference to the Messiah.[42]

Therefore, it was not just any messenger of YHWH, but rather, The Messenger of YHWH, The Messiah. The Scriptures then record that YHWH, not the Messenger of YHWH, saw that Mosheh turned aside to see and Elohim called to him from the midst of the bush. Elohim called "*Mosheh! Mosheh!*" Most people read over this part without much thought as to why Elohim said Mosheh's name twice. One explanation is that it was written twice to emphasize how loud it was spoken. This is certainly a plausible, and likely correct explanation.

Another explanation which is equally plausible is provided in the clear reading of the text as we see Elohim, which is the plural reference to the Almighty, manifesting Himself as both The Messiah and YHWH and both called out to Mosheh. That is why, the name Mosheh was said twice, it was spoken by YHWH and The Messiah.

Elohim then introduced Himself to Mosheh by stating: "*I am the Elohim of your father, the Elohim of Abraham, the Elohim of Yitshaq, and the Elohim of Ya'akov.*" The interesting thing about this introduction from the Almighty is that it appears that Mosheh did not know the Name of YHWH, despite the fact that  Abraham, Yitshaq and Ya'akov knew the Name. Apparently, during the time that the Hebrews (Ibrim)[43] were in Mitsrayim, they forgot the Name of YHWH or did not use the Name. If they did, chances are very good

that Pharaoh would have known the Name, since the Hebrews constituted a large portion of his kingdom. Yet later in the Scriptures Pharaoh states: *"Who is YHWH, that I should obey His voice to let Yisra'el go? I do not know YHWH, nor am I going to let Yisra'el go."* Shemot 5:2. Since Mosheh was raised in Pharaoh's household he may not have known the Name.

As a result, Mosheh had to ask the question: *"See, when I come to the children of Yisra'el and say to them, 'The Elohim of your fathers has sent me to you,' and they say to me, 'What is His Name?' what shall I say to them?' In response, Elohim said to Mosheh, 'I AM THAT WHICH I AM' and He said, 'Thus you shall say to the children of Yisra'el, I AM has sent me to you.'"* Shemot 3:13-14.

The Hebrew translation for "I AM THAT WHICH I AM" is 'eyah asher eyah' (אהיה אשר אהיה). This is the Name of the Almighty which defines His eternal nature, it is a descriptive Name with which YHWH uses to refer to Himself in the first person. Only YHWH can use the Name "I EXIST" or "I AM." All others must refer to Him in the third person and in the next verse He provides His Name as a proper noun in the third person.

Elohim continued His introduction to Mosheh as follows: *"Thus you are to say to the children of Yisra'el, YHWH Elohi* (יהוה אלהי) *of your fathers the Elohi of Abraham, the Elohi of Yitshaq and the Elohi of Ya'akov has sent me to you. This is My Name forever, and this is My remembrance to all generations."* Shemot 3:15. Notice how YHWH first describes Himself to Mosheh in the first person and then He provides His Name in the third person.

A definition of the Name YHWH can be gleaned from the ancient pictographs which originally were used in the Hebrew language. Remember that the earliest representation of the Name would have looked something like this: 𐤑𐤉𐤑𐤋. The yud (𐤋)represented by an arm and a hand means: "to make or work." The hey (𐤑) represented by a person with raised hands means: "behold or to reveal." The vav (𐤉) represented by a nail or a peg means: "to add or secure." A very rudimentary interpretation of these symbols could be: "The Maker of all that exists" or "In His hand is all that exists" or "He causes to become." There are other possible interpretations which would require a completely separate study. Prayer and meditation on the Name is an extremely valuable practice as we shall see.

An important aspect of the Name according to YHWH is that it is His " . . . *remembrance (memorial) to all generations.*" King David (Dawid)[44] uses this same reference in the Psalms (Tehillim).[45] "*O, YHWH, your Name is forever, O YHWH, your remembrance to all generations.*" Tehillim 135:13. Again he states: "*[12] But You, O YHWH, shall endure forever, and the remembrance of Your Name to all generations. [13] You will arise and have mercy on Tzion; for the time to favor her, yes, the set time, has come. [14] For Your servants take pleasure in her stones, and show favor to her dust.[15] So the nations shall fear the Name of YHWH, and all the kings of the earth Your glory. [16] For YHWH shall build up Tzion; He shall appear in His glory.[17] He shall regard the prayer of the destitute, and shall not despise their prayer. [18] This will be written for the generation to come, that a people yet to be created may praise YHWH.*" Tehillim 102:12-18. From both of these passages it is clear that YHWH has given us His Name

forever as a memorial; this is how we are to remember Him.

I want to digress for a moment because this notion of the Name being a memorial or a remembrance deserves some attention before we proceed any further. The prophet Malachi actually references a Book of Remembrance more accurately described as a Sefer Zikarone (ספר זכרון). *"16 Then those who feared YHWH spoke to one another, and YHWH listened and heard them; so a book of remembrance (Sefer Zikarone) was written before Him for those who fear YHWH and who meditate on His Name. 17 'They shall be Mine,' says YHWH of hosts, 'On the day that I make them My jewels. And I will spare them as a man spares his own son who serves him.' 18 Then you shall again discern between the righteous and the wicked, between one who serves Elohim and one who does not serve Him."* Malachi 3:16-18.

It is clear from this passage that YHWH keeps a memorial or record of those who fear Him *and meditate on His Name.* Those individuals included in this record are categorized as righteous, servants and sons. Could this be the same Sefer as the one commonly referred to as "The Lamb's Book of Life" more accurately described as the Sefer Chayiym (ספר חיים) – The Scroll of the Living? Look at how King Dawid refers to this Scroll of the Living when speaking of his adversaries: *"May they be blotted out of the book (scroll) of life and not be listed with the righteous."* Tehillim 69:28 NIV. He speaks of his enemies names being blotted out of the Scroll. This was also referred to by the Messiah concerning the faithful: *"He who overcomes shall be clothed in white garments, and I will not blot out his name from the Book of Life; but I will confess his name before*

My Father and before His angels." Revelation 3:5 NKJV. Both of these Scrolls include the names of the righteous.

I hope that this fact alone demonstrates the importance that YHWH places on names. These Scrolls contain names - not photos, fingerprints, numbers or any other form of identification. If you still do not think that names are important then maybe you would not mind if your name was blotted out or replaced with some one else's, or even some nickname that someone else gave you. I am certain that you would not want that and neither would I - I want my name in that Scroll and I want it put in there correctly. Some day when the Scrolls are opened and judgment is rendered (Daniel 7:10) everyone will understand the importance of names. The Scroll of Remembrance is for those who dwell upon the Name of YHWH, something which is difficult for someone who does not know or use the Name.

Now back to our discussion of the Sefer Shemot. After the initial introduction between YHWH and Mosheh we read the following: "*2 Elohim also said to Mosheh, I AM YHWH. 3 I appeared to Abraham, to Yitshaq and to Ya'akov as El Shaddai, but by My Name YHWH I did not make myself known to them. 4 I also established my covenant with them to give them the*

land of Canaan, where they lived as aliens. 5 Moreover, I have heard the groaning of the Yisra'elites, whom the Mitsrites are enslaving, and I have remembered my covenant. 6 Therefore, say to the Yisra'elites: I AM YHWH, and I will bring you out from under the yoke of the Mitsrites. I will free you from being slaves

to them, and I will redeem you with an outstretched arm and with mighty acts of judgment. 7 I will take you as my own people, and I will be your Elohim. Then you will know that I am YHWH your Elohim, who brought you out from under the yoke of the Mitsrites. 8 And I will bring you to the land I swore with uplifted hand to give to Abraham, to Yitshaq and to Ya'akov. I will give it to you as a possession. I am YHWH." Shemot 6:2-8.

This passage seems to contradict previous accounts in the Sefer Beresheet where the Patriarchs knew and used the Name of YHWH. Upon further investigation it appears that while they knew the Name, they did not understand the depth of the meaning of what YHWH was trying to impart through that Name, nor did they receive a complete revelation of the Name. While they understood YHWH as El Shaddai, they had not yet seen the full manifestation of YHWH.

The sage Maimonides, also known as Rambam, contends that the Name El Shaddai describes Elohim when He performs miracles that do not openly disrupt the normal course of nature. This was the way the Patriarchs perceived Elohim when He assured their survival in times of famine, made them victorious  over physically superior enemies, and gave them extraordinary success in amassing wealth. Though miraculous, none of the above openly violated the laws of nature. Thus the Patriarchs had only seen YHWH manifest Himself as El Shaddai. Mosheh however, would soon witness miracles of a magnitude that dwarfed

anything the Patriarchs had ever seen. While this seems plausible it does not take into account the judgment that Abraham witnessed as fire and brimstone fell upon the cities of Sodom, Gomorrah, Admah and Zeboiim. To this very day you can pick up pieces of brimstone in these desolate cities which remain a testimony of the judgment of YHWH.

The Sage Rashi explains that YHWH, the Name revealed to Mosheh, represents Elohim as the One Who carries out His promises, for Elohim was now prepared to fulfill His pledge to free Yisra'el and bring them to the Land. While the Patriarchs were told that Elohim's Name was YHWH, they had not seen Him in practice as having kept His promise, for the time had not yet come for the Land to be given to

them. Nevertheless, they had perfect faith that when the proper time arrived, He would do so. Further, the Sage HaChaim comments that Elohim's essence is represented by the Name YHWH. Even though the Patriarchs knew the Name YHWH, only Mosheh had the degree of prophecy that enabled him to comprehend its significance to the highest degree possible for man.[46]

Another explanation for the apparent contradiction is that the translation is incorrect. While most translations read ". . . *by My Name YHWH I did not make myself known to them*," an equally plausible translation could read "...*by My Name YHWH, was I not known to them?*" This passage could be a rhetorical question intended to emphasize the fact that the Name was known by the predecessors of

Mosheh.

From what we read in the Scriptures, Mosheh, the chosen deliverer of Yisra'el, one of the elect of Elohim, spent up to two thirds of his life not knowing the Elohim of Yisra'el, or even His Name. This is the same condition in which numerous Elect now find themselves. Many who are called and chosen do not know the Name of the One they worship nor do they know how to pronounce the Name. There are also many people who are currently restoring the Name of YHWH into their worship. They realize that they have been using impersonal and incorrect titles to worship their Elohim and they desire to restore the Name to its proper place.

The Name clearly was spoken in the past, it will be spoken in the future and, likewise, it is supposed to be spoken in the present. Just because mankind has been deceived for centuries does not mean that we are supposed to give up or admit defeat, especially on such an important point. To the contrary, we should heed the words of the Messiah when He said: "7 Ask, and it will be given to you; seek, and you will find; knock, and it will be opened to you. 8 For everyone who asks receives, and he who seeks finds, and to him who knocks it will be opened." Matthew (Mattityahu) 7:7-8 NKJV. We are called to persevere and overcome so that our names are not blotted out. Part of our journey is to know, use and meditate upon the Name. If you truly desire to succeed in this regard then all you need to do is ask.

8

The Third Commandment

Some people cite the Third commandment as the reason for not speaking the Name. Sadly, the Third Commandment was intended to regulate the proper use of the Name, not abolish the use of the Name. The Third Commandment states: "*You shall not take the name of YHWH your Elohim in vain, for YHWH will not hold him guiltless who takes His name in vain.*" Shemot 20:7.

The Hebrew word for "vain" is shaw (שׁוא) which is used in the sense of "emptiness, desolation, lying, nothingness, uselessness or misuse." Therefore, the Third Commandment is telling us to use the Name, but not to abuse the Name or bring it to naught. The Scriptures clearly reveal that the Name was properly used after the Ten Commandments were given to the Children of Yisra'el, so there is absolutely no evidence to support the notion that the Name was not to be used.

How incongruous to think that YHWH would go through all the trouble to reveal His Name to Yisra'el only to turn around and command them not to use His Name. The Name is found two times in this one commandment so you have to say the Name if you want to recite the

commandment. In fact, the First Commandment is a declaration of the Name. *"I am YHWH your Elohim, who brought you out of the land of Mitsrayim, out of the house of bondage."* Shemot 20:2. Clearly the Name was meant to be spoken.

Another amazing truth in the Third commandment is the existence of the Aleph Taw (את)[47] three times in one verse. The Messiah is present in this commandment which makes perfect sense because He said: *"I have come in My Father's Name . . ."* John (Yahanan) 5:43 NIV.

There are other passages in the Torah regulating the use of the Name. For instance: *"you shall not swear by My Name falsely, nor shall you profane the Name of your Elohim: I am YHWH."* Vayiqra 19:12. Notice that the Scriptures do not forbid people from swearing by the Name, only swearing by the Name falsely.[48] This verse contains an את embedded within the Hebrew text as well as in the following text: *"31 Keep my commands and follow them. I am YHWH. 32 Do not profane My Set Apart Name. I must be acknowledged as set apart by the Yisra'elites. I am YHWH, who makes you set apart 33 and who brought you out of Mitsrayim to be your Elohim. I am YHWH."* Vayiqra 22:31-23:1. The Hebrew word for profane is halal (חלל) which means: "to wound, to dissolve; figuratively, to profane."

To demonstrate the severity of these warnings we can read about an instance when someone blasphemed the Name of YHWH in the camp of Yisra'el. *"10 Now the son*

of an Yisra'elite woman, whose father was a Mitsrite, went out among the children of Yisra'el; and this Yisra'elite woman's son and a man of Yisra'el fought each other in the camp. [11] And the Yisra'elite woman's son blasphemed the Name of YHWH and cursed; and so they brought him to Mosheh. (His mother's name was Shelomith the daughter of Dibri, of the tribe of Dan.) [12] Then they put him in custody, that the mind of YHWH might be shown to them. [13] And YHWH spoke to Mosheh, saying, [14] 'Take outside the camp him who has cursed; then let all who heard him lay their hands on his head, and let all the congregation stone him. [15] Then you shall speak to the children of Yisra'el, saying: 'Whoever curses his Elohim shall bear his transgression.''" Vayiqra 24:10-15.

Some have used this passage to justify not speaking the Name although a closer look at the text reveals that blasphemy is synonymous with cursing the Name, or using the Name to curse others. Nowhere do these verses suggest that using the Name of YHWH is, in itself, the act of blasphemy. That is pure religious tradition which is both unscriptural and dangerous in so much as it stifles the true Good News being carried to the nations, that is sealed in the Names of the Father and His Son.

Yisra'el, the Chosen People of YHWH, was not chosen because they were better than any of the other nations. Rather they were chosen for a purpose. That purpose was to be set apart from the rest of the world and demonstrate to the Nations how to live righteous lives according to the instructions of YHWH. They were supposed to bring esteem to the Name and lift it up as a banner to the Nations. Instead, the opposite has occurred and we can see the truth in the prophesy of Yirmeyahu

who declared: "O YHWH, *my strength and my fortress, My refuge in the day of affliction, The Nations shall come to You from the ends of the earth and say, 'Surely our fathers have inherited lies, worthlessness and unprofitable things.'"* Yirmeyahu 16:19.

Aside from the Third Commandment which directs us not to bring the Name to naught, there is actually a curse for not revering the Name. "*58 If you do not carefully follow all the words of this Torah, which are written in this scroll, and do not revere this glorious and awesome Name - YHWH your Elohim - 59 YHWH will send fearful plagues on you and your descendants, harsh and prolonged disasters, and severe and lingering illnesses. 60 He will bring upon you all the diseases of Mitsrayim that you dreaded, and they will cling to you. 61 YHWH will also bring on you every kind of sickness and disaster not recorded in this scroll of the Torah, until you are destroyed. 62 You who were as numerous as the stars in the sky will be left but few in number, because you did not obey YHWH your Elohim. 63 Just as it pleased YHWH to make you prosper and increase in number, so it will please him to ruin and destroy you. You will be uprooted from the land you are entering to possess.*" Devarim 28:58-63.

YHWH gave this warning to Yisra'el, but it applies to anyone who has entered into covenant with Him. We see that Yisra'el has, in fact, suffered the consequences of profaning His Name. (Yirmeyahu 12:17-17). In Devarim 4:2 the Yisra'elites are instructed "*Do not add to the Word which I commanded you, and do not take away from it, so as to guard the commands of YHWH your Elohim which I am commanding you.*" Again in Devarim 12:32 the Yisra'elites are told "*All the words I am commanding you,*

guard to do it - do not add nor take away from it." (see also Mishle 30:6; Revelation 22:18-19).

Regrettably, both Judaism and Christianity are guilty of altering, removing, replacing and adding to the Scriptures - especially when it comes to referencing the Name of YHWH. I do not care how they try to excuse or justify their actions - we were explicitly commanded against committing this very sin. The revelation of the Name of YHWH and the identity and work of the Son are arguably some of the most important and foundational truths contained within the Scriptures. If you do not <u>know</u> the Name of the Mighty One that you serve, how can you really be sure who you serve and how can you fully share your faith and belief with others.

According to the Prophet Malachi: *"For from the rising of the sun, even to its going down, My Name shall be great among the Nations; in every place incense shall be offered to My Name, and a pure offering; for My Name shall be great among the Nations, says YHWH of hosts."* Malachi 1:11.

It is now time to see the fulfillment of this prophesy as the Nations, who are the goyim (גוֹיִם) or the heathen, start to hear and learn the Name of YHWH. This will not happen unless the people of YHWH start searching out and declaring His Name. *"Therefore behold, I will this once cause them to know, I will cause them to know My hand and My might; and they shall know that My Name is YHWH."* Yirmeyahu 16:21.

Once again, the Aleph Taw (את) is embedded in two places in this single passage between "cause them to know" את "my hand" את "my might." The Messiah is not merely exalted to the right hand of YHWH (Acts 7:55,

Ibrim 12:2) but He is "the Right hand" of YHWH.
(Tehillim 17:7; 60:5; 108:6). With that understanding we
can discern from the prophesy that The Messiah will
reveal the Name which is absolutely consistent with the
mission of The Messiah as we read in the "New
Testament" or rather the Messianic Scriptures.[49]

I suggest that you follow the lead of Joshua
(Yahushua)[50] when he spoke to Yisra'el before entering
the promised land. *"14 Now fear YHWH and serve him with
all faithfulness. Throw away the gods your forefathers
worshiped beyond the River and in Mitsrayim, and serve
YHWH. 15 But if serving YHWH seems undesirable to you,
then choose for yourselves this day whom you will serve, whether
the gods your forefathers served beyond the River, or the gods of
the Amorites, in whose land you are living. But as for me and my
household, we will serve YHWH." Yahushua 24:14-15.* If we
choose to serve YHWH then we should determine to use
His Name.

9

The Name of the Son

The mention of the name of Joshua leads us naturally to the Name of the Son because they are, in fact, the same. But before we examine the name of Joshua I would like to look in the Tanakh to see if we are given any clues as to the Name of the Son, also known as the Messiah.[51] There are numerous prophecies that refer to the Messiah as "The Branch" (Yeshayahu 4:2, 11:1, Zekaryah 3:8, 6:12). In Tehillim the word branch and son are even mixed in certain translations because the meaning is so clear. For instance, look at how The Amplified Version translates Tehillim 80:15: "*[Protect and maintain] the stock which Your right hand planted, and the branch (the son) that You have reared and made strong for Yourself.*"

The prophecies of Yirmeyahu give us a clue as to the Name of the Branch. "*⁵ Behold, the days are coming, says YHWH, That I will raise to David a Branch of righteousness; a King shall reign and prosper, and execute judgment and righteousness in the earth. ⁶ In His days Yahudah will be saved, and Yisra'el will dwell safely; Now this is His Name by which He will be called: YHWH OUR RIGHTEOUSNESS.*" Yirmeyahu 23:5-6 (see also 33:16).

This does not mean that the full Name of the

Messiah will actually be "YHWH Tsadikeenu" which is the transliteration of יהוה צדקנו, rather it provides a hint of His character. The Hebrew name that means "YHWH our righteousness" is Yahuzadak (יהוצדק) – YHWH (is our) Tzadik (righteous). This is an important link to the Name of the Messiah. In many modern English translations they incorrectly transliterate this name as Jehozadak but remember, there is no "J" sound in Hebrew.

We are now ready for the final piece in the puzzle which is provided by the Prophet Zekaryah. *"11 Take the silver and gold and make a crown, and set it on the head of the high priest, Joshua son of Yahuzadak (יהוצדק). 12 Tell him this is what YHWH of Hosts says: 'Here is the man whose name is the Branch, and He will branch out from his place and build the temple of YHWH. 13 It is He who will build the temple of YHWH, and He will be clothed with majesty and will sit and rule on his throne. And He will be a priest on his throne. And there will be harmony between the two.'"* Zekaryah 6:11-13.

This prophesy is profound because it not only provides a key to the Name of the Messiah, but it also describes what the Messiah will do: He will build the Temple and sit as King and High Priest – this is the Melek (King) Tzadik (Righteous) that we read of in the Torah,[52] and Zekaryah tells us prophetically that His Name will be Joshua son of Yahuzadak (יהוצדק) or rather Yahushua the son of YHWH our righteousness.

So then, the Name of the Messiah is the same name as Joshua, the commander of Yisra'el who began as a servant and later led the children of Yisra'el across the

Jordan River[53] into the promised land. The one who directed their circumcision[54] and who led them into battle as they conquered their enemies.[55] How appropriate that the Messiah of Yisra'el would bear the  same Name as this great patriarch. We have already seen that Joshua is not an accurate transliteration although before we extrapolate further on that point we will first review the overwhelming agreement concerning the connection between the name of the patriarch commonly called "Joshua" and the Name of the Messiah.

The following is a sample of what some religious scholars have written concerning the Name of the Messiah: "In Hebrew it is the same as Joshua. In two places [Acts 7:45 and Hebrews 4:8] in the New Testament [Jesus] is used where it means Joshua, the leader of the [Yisraelites] into Canaan, and in our translation the name Joshua should have been retained."[56] "Jesus - This is the regular Greek translation of the Hebrew Joshua."[57] "Jesus Christ - The name Jesus means Savior, and was a common name, derived from the ancient Hebrew Jehoshua."[58] "Jesus - The Greek form of the name Joshua or Jeshua. Jeshua - Yahweh is Salvation or Yahweh is opulence."[59] "Jesus - The same name as Joshua, the former deliverer of Israel."[60]

Now take a look at some secular references: "Jesus Christ - Although Matthew (1:21) interprets the name originally Joshua, that is, 'Yahweh is Salvation,' and finds it specially appropriate for Jesus of Nazareth, it was a common one at that time."[61] "Jesus Christ - . . . the

customary Greek form for the common Hebrew name Joshua."[62]

The scholars, both religious and secular, are in agreement that the name of the man commonly referred to as Joshua son of Nun, is the same name as the Hebrew Messiah, traditionally called Jesus. Sadly, through most English translations there is no apparent connection between these two names although once we start correcting inherited errors, the relationship becomes evident.

The common Hebrew spelling of the name Joshua is יהושע and the typical transliterated spelling in English is Yehoshua, Yahushua, Yahoshua or Yahshua.

The Scriptures record that Mosheh changed Yahushua's name from Hoshea (Bemidbar 13:16). This is a very important event because whenever you see someone receive a name change in the Scriptures it is a red flag for a very important turning point in a person's life. In the case of Yahushua, son of Nun, we read that his name was originally Hoshea (הושע) which simply means "salvation" or "deliverer." "He was Hoshea only ("he will save") up to his noble witness after spying Canaan. Henceforth, [YHWH's] name is prefixed, '[YHWH] by him would save Israel' [Bemidbar 13:16]. Son of Nun, of Ephraim (1 Chronicles 7:27). This forms the contrast in the Antitype found in the Messiah (Matthew 1:21), 'you shall call His name [Yahushua], for He shall save His people from their trespasses.'"[63]

So then, we can confirm that the Name of the Messiah was to be the same Name as the Patriarch commonly called Joshua. The first time that we see the

Name of the Messiah in the Messianic Scriptures is in the Good News according to Matthew (Mattityahu)[64] as follows: "*[18] But the birth of* יהושע *[Yahushua] Messiah was as follows: After His mother Miryam was engaged to Yoseph, before they came together, she was found to be pregnant from the Set-apart Spirit. [19] And Yoseph her husband, being righteous, and not wishing to make a show of her, had in mind to put her away secretly.[20] But while he thought about this, see, a messenger of* יהוה *appeared to him in a dream, saying, 'Yoseph, son of Dawid, do not be afraid to take Miryam as your wife, for that which is in her was brought forth from the Set-apart Spirit.[21] And she shall give birth to a Son, and you shall call His Name* יהושע *[Yahushua] for He shall save His people from their sins.' [22] And all this came to be in order to fill what was spoken by* יהוה *through the prophet, saying [23] 'See, a maiden shall conceive, and she shall give birth to a Son, and they shall call His Name Immanu'el,' which translated, means 'El with us.' [24] And Yoseph, awaking from his sleep, did as the messenger of* יהוה *commanded him and took his wife, [25] but knew her not until she gave birth to her Son, the first-born. And he called His Name* יהושע *[Yahushua]."* Mattityahu 1:18-25 The Scriptures (transliterated Name of the Messiah added for clarity).

Sadly, you will not find this rendering in most modern English translations which derive from Greek manuscripts that have been Hellenized and actually replaced the true Name of the Messiah with the fabricated name – Jesus. This subject will be discussed at length in the next chapter but for now we will focus on the Hebrew Name of the Messiah. The important point that I want to emphasize is the definition of the Name provided in the

text – *"for He will save His people from their transgressions."*

According to Brown-Driver-Briggs Hebrew and English Lexicon the Name Yahushua (יהושע, יהושע), later Yahshua (ישוע) means "YHWH is salvation." Notice that with Yahushua, son of Nun, the Name means that YHWH will save His people, while with Yahushua the Messiah the Name means <u>He</u> (YHWH) will save His people, identifying Yahushua directly with YHWH.

Once we discover the True Name of the Son, as with the Name of the Father, we then desire the correct pronunciation. As we have seen, the Name of the Father is יהוה. The Hebrew word for "salvation" is ישוע and the Hebrew word for "will save" is יושיע. These three provide the basic roots for the Name of the Messiah which is spelled יהושע. It is interesting to note that both the Name of the Father and the Name of the Son start with the same three root letters yud (י) hey (ה) vav (ו) or יהו.

This is significant because in the Hebrew language when words share a root it signifies a connection between them. Further, this would lead me to believe that the Name of the Son sounds like the Name of the Father. That is why I like to transliterate the Name of the Son as Yahushua, because it emphasizes the Name of the Father. The Scriptures tell us that the Name of the Son means "He saves His people" and they further reveal that He is Immanuel, "El with us" (Yeshayahu 7:14; 8:8) Since we know that it is Yah that saves His people it only makes sense that we pronounce the Name as Yahushua.

As with the Name of the Father, the pronunciation can be a point of disagreement and contention. Some of the

common spellings currently used are: Yahushua, Yehoshua, Yahshua, Yahusha, Yeshua and Y'shua. One thing is certain, the Messiah did not speak English when He was on earth 2,000 years ago because the English language did not exist, nor did He write His Name in English for us to discover centuries later when the English language was developed. As a result, there is no sure way of knowing how to transliterate His Name into English and it is important not to get too caught up in the exact English spelling since it is only a transliteration to assist us in correctly pronouncing His Hebrew Name. I usually spell the Name of Messiah as Yahushua because it is consistent with the way that I pronounce YHWH.

Currently, a very popular spelling in the Messianic Community is Yeshua. They do this because they transliterate the Hebrew word for salvation (יֵשׁוּעַ) as yeshua. This usage also derives from the fact that the short form of Yahushua was יֵשׁוּעַ after the time of the Babylonian captivity (see Nehemyah 8:17). This short form spelling removed the ה and the ו which were a significant part of the Name of YHWH. Regardless, the short form name should still have the Yah sound at the beginning.

Thus יֵשׁוּעַ should be pronounced Yahshua. I see no reason for spelling it or pronouncing it as Yeshua, especially when it comes from the root יֵשַׁע which is pronounced yasha and means "deliver." It is perfectly acceptable to pronounce the Hebrew word יֵשׁוּעַ as yashua and the short form of Yahushua is more accurately rendered as Yahshua. This is important because however

you are going to refer to the Father, you should be consistent in how you refer to the Son, because the Son's Name comes from the Father's.

Messiah Yahushua specifically said: "*I have come in My Father's Name and with His power.*" John (Yahanan) 5:43. The Greek word for "in" is *en* (εν) which according to Thayer's Greek Lexicon can mean "in, on, at, with, by, among." Therefore, Yahushua could have been saying that He came with His Father's Name. All evidence certainly points to the Messiah having the Name of the Father. (Shemot 23:20-21; 32:34 and 33:14; Yeshayahu 63:9). As a result, by spelling the Messiah's Name with "yeh" rather than "Yah" you may be suppressing the Name of YHWH which is intended to be revealed through the Name of the Messiah.

Another reason why I tend to avoid the spelling Yeshua is due to the Rabbinic acronym Ye.sh.u (יש״ו) which stands for <u>y</u>imach <u>sh</u>emo <u>v</u>ezichro ימח שמו וזכרו and means "may his name and memory be blotted out." Historically, there has been considerable and well documented hostility toward Yahushua from a number of prominent Rabbis. There are also Talmudic references to a bastard child named Yeshu (a.k.a. Ben Stada), the son of an Israelite woman named Miriam (Mary) who was betrothed to a carpenter. The Talmud describes this man as a sorcerer, a heretic and a "mamzer," which is a bastard.

It also describes him as a "niddah," a child conceived during his mothers' menstruation period. This Yeshu was executed on the eve of Passover, as was the Messiah. While there is debate over whether Yeshu is a direct reference to Yahushua, I believe that it is consistent

with the ancient Rabbinic practice of attacking, degrading and attempting to hide Yahushua, the Messiah, from the Jews. In fact, there was a Rabbinic tradition which referred to the Gospels, pronounced evangelion in Greek, as "aven-gilyon" in Hebrew which means "falsehood of blank paper" or "avon-gilyon" in Hebrew which means "revelation of sin."[65] I try to avoid anything even remotely related to this type of malicious and deceptive teaching.

Therefore, I prefer Yahushua and suggest emphasizing the Name "Yah" when referring to the Messiah. The spelling difference in English is minor and it is the pronunciation which counts.

Ultimately, I am not going to quibble with somebody over how they transliterate יהושע into English, I am more concerned that they discontinue the habit of calling the Messiah by an incorrect Hellenized Greek name which has its origins in pagan sun god worship. I view these differences the same as accent differences between people of difference cultures. If you meet with Believers throughout the world they all speak different languages and with different accents.

We now see flocks of people from around the world returning to the true Name of the Father and the Son. These Names have been forgotten for centuries and people are now struggling to get the exact pronunciation, which is absolutely important although it should not become a point of contention between Believers. Rather, we should all endeavor to seek the truth and *"work out our own yashua (salvation) with fear and trembling"* (Philippians 2:12) and remember that forgiveness comes through faith in the

Name. *"To this One all the prophets bear witness, that through His Name, everyone believing in Him does receive forgiveness of transgressions."* Acts 10:43

The Name of the Son was actually hinted throughout the Tanakh over 300 times. Since the Hebrew word for "salvation" is yashua, most places where the Scriptures speak of YHWH's salvation it says "yashua." For instance, Shemot 15:2 says: *"Yah is my strength and my song He has become my yashua (יְשׁוּעָה)."*

Every time the salvation or deliverance of YHWH is referred to in the Tanakh it is a reference to the Messiah - Yahushua and when a person reads the Hebrew text concerning the promised Messiah, they read and are familiar with the name Yahushua which is usually what the Scriptures are referring to: Yah saving His people. What they do not read is the Hellenized Greek name "Jesus" which has no real connection to the Hebrew Messiah, other than the fact that millions of unwitting Christians and Catholics have been taught to use this inherited "nickname" while referring to the Messiah of Yisra'el.

Let us look at how the Name of the Messiah is embedded within the Hebrew Scriptures:

> *"8 He shall swallow up death forever, and the Master YHWH shall wipe away tears from all faces, and take away the reproach of His people from all the earth. For YHWH has spoken. 9 And it shall be said in that day, 'See, this is our Elohim. We have waited for Him, and He saves us. This is YHWH; we have waited for Him, let us be glad and rejoice in His*

salvation.'" Yeshayahu 25:8-9.

To anyone who reads the last verse in Hebrew they will understand it to read *"And it will be said in that day: 'Behold, this is our Elohim; we have waited for Him, and He will save us. This is YHWH; we have waited for Him; we will be glad and rejoice in His yashua."* Remember the yashua of YHWH is Yahushua.

Let us take a look at another example: *"Thus says YHWH: 'Keep justice, and do righteousness, for My salvation is about to come, and My righteousness to be revealed.'"* Yeshayahu 56:1. A person reading this in Hebrew would hear: *"Keep justice, and do righteousness, for My yashua (yashuatee) is about to come, and My righteousness to be revealed."*

This is powerful. The Tanakh is filled with hints of the Hebrew Name of the Messiah. So you see that those of Hebrew descent who read and understand the Scriptures are waiting for the Messiah who will be called "YHWH their Salvation" – Yahushua while the Christian Church for centuries has been trying to present them with a Hellenized Greek Messiah named Jesus. There is absolutely no connection between these names, etymologically or otherwise. No wonder they are not accepting the Christian gospel, the Christian Messiah named Jesus does not fit the prophesies.

Jesus was not and is not the name of the Hebrew Messiah, but if you tell a Hebrew individual that the Messiah is named Yahushua, it should make perfect sense to them. If you want to start seeing Jews find their Messiah, start showing them the real Messiah - Yahushua.

10

Jesus

The Scriptures record that: *"everyone who calls on the Name of YHWH will be saved."* (Yoel 2:32). This leads us directly to the Name of the Son which, contrary to popular belief, is not, Jesus. This may seem like a quite shocking statement to any Christian who has staked their faith and salvation on the name of Jesus, I know it was to me at first.

You see Jesus is the English version of the Hellenized Greek name Iesous, spelled Iesus in Latin. Some say that this name has no specific meaning, while others indicate that it refers to different pagan deities. One thing is for certain, Jesus was not a Hebrew name nor is it a translation of the Hebrew Name Yahushua. Notice that the English name Jesus is not even a transliteration of the Greek or Latin spellings because it starts with a "J" sound. The Messiah was definitely not called Jesus nor was that name ever spoken while He walked the Earth. There was and is no letter "J" in either the Hebrew or Aramaic languages, nor was there a letter "J" in the Greek alphabet. None of these languages even contain the "J" sound in their vocabulary.

Any time you see a "J" in an English translation of a Hebrew or Aramaic transcript it should be given the "Y"

sound and any time you see a "J" in an English translation of a Greek manuscript it should be given an "I" sound. In fact, the letter "J" with the unique and specific "J" sound did not exist in any language until the 15ᵗʰ Century. It is a fairly new addition to the linguistic world yet it has been littered throughout ancient Scriptural translations erroneously perverting the names of Prophets, Sages and most importantly the Father and the Son.

Since there was no letter "J" in the Hebrew language it does not even make sense to call the Messiah Jesus. The name Jesus has only been in existence since the year 1559 AD. As a result, it is important to look deeper into the roots of the name Jesus to see how the name and nature of the Savior was changed. There is no authoritative source which claims that the name Jesus or Iesous was the original name of the Hebrew Messiah. To the contrary, they all validate the fact that the true name derives from Yahushua.

While the traditional English, Greek and Latin names for the Messiah bear little resemblance to His correct Hebrew Name there are striking similarities to the  names of pagan deities. In fact some claim that they are directly related to the name Iaso, also spelled Ieso, who was the Greek goddess of healing, who is intimately related to sun god worship. In fact, according to Greek mythology, the father of Ieso was Asclepius, the deity of healing. His father was Apollo, the sun god. "Iaso is Ieso in the Ionic dialect of the Greeks, Iesous being the contracted genitive form. In

David Kravitz's, *Dictionary of Greek and Roman Mythology*, we find a similar form, namely Iasus. There are four different Greek deities with the name Iasus, one of them being the Son of Rhea."[66]

There is significant proof that Iesous is linked to the mystery cult of the pagan god Dionysus, a savior god, whose father was Zeus, the Greek sun god.  According, to mythology Zeus also had sons named Iasus, Iasion and Iasius, all who were considered to be "sons of god." There is also a relationship to the Egyptian goddess Isis and her son Isu. "According to Reallexikon der Agpyptischen Religionsgeschichte, the name of Isis appears in hieroglyphic inscriptions as ESU or ES. Isu and Esu sound exactly like "Jesu" that the Savior is called in the translated Scriptures of many languages. Esus was a Gallic deity comparable to the Scandinavian Odin. The Greek abbreviation for Iesous is IHS, which is found on many inscriptions made by the "Church" during the Middle Ages. IHS was the mystery name for Bacchus (Tammuz) [Dionysus] another sun-deity."[67]

I remember as a child seeing IHS adorned on various furniture and religious items in the mainstream Protestant Church that I attended. I never knew what it  meant and I doubt that anybody in the congregation knew that it was related to pagan sun worship. Therefore we see Christianity directly identifying their Savior with mythical sun deities. It is out in the open for anybody to see, but nobody recognizes the connection because these are simply inherited traditions

whose true meaning has been obscured through time, ignorance and misinformation.

Speaking of inherited traditions with pagan origins, Bacchus was also known as Ichthus the Fish which is the source of the fish symbol commonly used in Christianity. Sadly, the fish symbol was a pagan religious icon long before Christianity adopted it as a symbol. In fact, in many cultures it represented the outline of the vulva  of the great mother goddess. Some have attempted to legitimize the use of the fish symbol by creating an anagram from the word ichthus as "Iesous CHristos Theo Uiou Soter" or rather "Iesous Christos God Son Savior."

Despite the numerous problems regarding the Greek names and titles in this acrostic, the question in my mind is: What is the point? Why would you make an anagram out of a pagan concept and incorporate it into your own worship? It would be like trying to find an anagram for the Greek word ofin (ὄφιν) which means "serpent" based upon the Scripture found in John (Yahanan) 3:14 *"And as Mosheh lifted up the serpent in the wilderness, even so must the Son of Man be lifted up."* It certainly would be simple enough to create an anagram out of the four Greek letters and then Christians could start displaying serpents on their Bibles, t-shirts, hats and bumper stickers as well as the fish. I hope that the absurdity of this example is evident. Sadly, it is not much different than incorporating the sign for Tammuz, the Tau popularly known as the cross, as the universal symbol for Christianity. The use of symbols which have pagan

origins and which are not expressly provided for in the Tanakh can be dangerous and misleading, but let us now return to the subject at hand, the name Jesus.

It is a well known fact that certain names in early compilations of Scriptures were altered or "Hellenized."[68] In other words, they were changed to ascribe the attribute or reflect the names of pagan deities. One of the most striking was that of Elijah (Eliyahu) whose name means "YHWH is Elohim." In an act of unbelievable ignorance and audacity, his name was replaced in most Greek New Testament manuscripts with the name of the sun god Helios. By doing this, translators removed the Name of YHWH, as well as the declaration that YHWH was Elohim, from the Scriptures and replaced it with the blasphemous name of a pagan sun god. If you get a hold of most any accepted Greek manuscript to this day and look at Mattityahu 17:11 you will read *"Helias surely shall come and restore all things."* I count at least 30 instances where the name of Helios is found in the Textus Receptus, the received Greek texts from which the New Testament derives. Interestingly the Hebrew version of Mattityahu does not contain this Hellenization or should I say - error.

I am at a loss for words to describe the gravity of this blunder. Sadly, this was not the only instance where names were Hellenized in the Scriptures and while most modern translations have corrected many of those mistakes, the Name of the Messiah has remained Hellenized. To this day you will still find the name Easter

in the King James Version in Acts 12:4 in place of the Appointed Time of Passover (Pesach). Easter is the pagan fertility goddess also known as "The Goddess of the Dawn" who is worshipped around the vernal equinox and through the process of syncretism, many Christians have unknowingly participated in her worship by holding Easter sunrise services.

It should now be abundantly clear to the reader that, as with the Name of the Father, so too, the Name of the Son has been altered and suppressed for centuries. In order to restore a right relationship between Elohim and His people, these Names must be restored. This is especially important in light of the fact that He calls those who obey Him His friends. It is hard to say that you are someone's friend if you do not even know their Name.

Many times in my life I have had conversations with people who would claim to know someone, only after further inquiry to discover that they did not even know the person's last name. In some instances I have had clients who did not even know a persons first or last name, only their "street name." There comes a point when you must question the depth or extent of a person's relationship when they do not even know certain important details about another.

Likewise, if you want to have a friendship with Yahushua it is going to have to involve more than just claiming that you know Him. *"14 You are My friends if you do whatever I command you.15 No longer do I call you servants, for a servant does not know what his master is doing; but I have called you friends, for all things that I heard from My Father I*

have made known to you.[16] *You did not choose Me, but I chose you and appointed you that you should go and bear fruit, and that your fruit should remain, that whatever you ask the Father in My Name He may give you.*" John (Yahanan) 15:14-16 NKJV.[69]

Your relationship with the Messiah involves much more than just claiming to know Him, especially when you use an incorrect name. I suggest using His True Name as a terrific place to start. It may be awkward at first to speak the Hebrew Name Yahushua instead of the Hellenized Greek name - Jesus. Changing old habits is never easy, but the rewards are well worth it and Yahushua will certainly appreciate you using His correct Name. Using someone's name rather than a title implies familiarity and friendship. Since Yahushua has called us His friends it seems that we should take the time and energy necessary to learn His Name and the Name of the Father and start using those Names in our worship and prayer.

In my opinion you demonstrate how much of a friend that you are by how you respond to this issue. I have heard people say that it is too difficult to pronounce the Hebrew while others have called this an insignificant issue. They claim that it is simply a matter of the heart and no matter whether they use a title, a mistranslated Greek name or the correct Hebrew, "God knows our heart." While this argument sounds nice, it is in direct contradiction with the Scriptures. Each person needs to prayerfully consider this issue because we will all be standing before The Judge some day and we need to be prepared to give a response.

I have also had people respond to this information by stating: "You're not going to take away my Jesus." The point is simply that I am not trying to take away anything that belongs to you - the Name of the Messiah belongs to no man. My job is to help restore the truth and if you want to know the truth you should be more than willing to throw away a lie. On the other hand, if the truth is not in you, then you will believe lies and you will hold on to them. The Scriptures are very clear on this point.

Many of us who grew up loving the Name Jesus have emotional attachments to that Name. I understand the difficulty of letting go, but this issue requires decisive action and we should be more attached to the Person, rather than the false name, and our desire to know Him should override our desire to cling to a false tradition.

To emphasize the importance of knowing and using the true Name of the Messiah let us look at the most quoted verse of Scripture in Christianity concerning salvation. *"For Elohim so loved the world that He gave His only begotten Son, that whoever believes in Him should not perish but have everlasting life."* John (Yahanan) 3:16. Probably every Christian in the world knows this passage by heart, but few could quote beyond that portion.

Let us read on: *"17 For Elohim did not send His Son into the world to condemn the world, but that the world through Him might be saved. 18 He who believes in Him is not condemned; but he who does not believe is condemned already, because he has not believed in the Name of the only begotten Son of Elohim."* John (Yahanan) 3:17-18. Belief in the Name is a critical aspect of salvation and redemption. Therefore, it is safe to say that you had better know, use and believe in the correct name of the Savior, rather than some man-made nickname with pagan origins.

The Scriptures clearly record that Yahushua came to fulfill prophesy relating to the salvation of the Gentiles. *"16 Yet He warned them not to make Him known, 17 that it might be fulfilled which was spoken by Isaiah [Yeshayahu] the prophet, saying: 18 'Behold! My Servant whom I have chosen, My Beloved in whom My soul is well pleased! I will put My Spirit upon Him, and He will declare justice to the Gentiles. 19 He will not quarrel nor cry out, nor will anyone hear His voice in the streets. 20 A bruised reed He will not break, and smoking flax He will not quench, till He sends forth justice to victory; 21 and in His Name Gentiles will trust.'"* Mattityahu 12:15-21 NKJV. The reason that Gentiles would trust in His Name is so that they might be saved. They cannot trust in His Name if they do not know His Name or the real meaning of His Name which specifically refers to YHWH, the source of their salvation.

Let us look at another passage of Scripture which shows how important the Name will be when we stand at judgment. *"21 Not everyone who says to Me 'Lord, Lord,' shall enter into the reign of the heavens, but he who is doing the desire of My Father in the heavens. 22 Many shall say to me in that day, 'Lord, Lord, have we not prophesied in Your Name, and cast out demons in Your Name, and done many mighty works in Your Name?' 23 And then I shall declare to them, 'I never knew you, depart from me, you who work lawlessness!'"* Mattithyahu 7:21-23.

This Scripture always used to puzzle me because I was not sure who the Messiah was speaking to. After all, what group consists of many people who claim to be

prophesying in His Name, casting out demons in His Name and doing mighty works in His Name, while calling Him Lord. It sounded a lot like Christians to me. In fact, there is no other large group of people that portend to call upon His Name, but do not really know or use His Name. Notice that He tells them that He never knew them. As previously mentioned, it is difficult to have a relationship with someone when you do not even know their name.

Ultimately, this large group of people is told to depart from the Messiah because they commit lawlessness. The Greek word for lawlessness is anomia (ανομια) which simply means – without the instructions or without Torah. This group of people who are told to depart from the presence of the Messiah refuse to follow the instructions found within the Torah which is exactly what Christianity has done through a misapplication of the doctrine of grace. As a result, we see Christianity as a religion full of lawless individuals who do not even know the Name of the Messiah. Many are doing acts which they believe will gain them entrance into the kingdom but they will be told by the Messiah to depart because He never knew them.

Now this is not to say that everyone that uses the Name *Jesus* is going to hell. The Almighty is rich in mercy and quick to forgive. He does not punish us for our ignorance, *"for all have transgressed and fall short . . ."* (Romans 3:23). What I am saying is that we have been warned that some day there will be many people calling Yahushua "Lord" who thought they knew Him, but they will be wrong. It is important that we know the Messiah and an important part of knowing Him is getting His

Name right.

By the way: what about all of those miracles, casting out of demons and prophesying? Many people ask how this could be happening using the name of Jesus if the name is incorrect. There are several possibilities, one being that the acts are simply wrong - the prophesies, the signs and the wonders may be false. We know that the Anti-Messiah (also known as the Anti-Christ and The Lawless One) and his false prophet will perform many signs, lying wonders and unrighteous deception. (Mattityahu 24:24; Mark 13:22). These acts will deceive many regardless of the warnings provided in the Scriptures.

In fact, those who do not love the truth will be given a strong delusion so that they might believe the lies. (2 Thessalonians 2:9-12). People often come to the incorrect conclusion that simply because they witness a sign, it must be from YHWH. They are setting themselves up for disaster because *a wicked and perverse generation which seeks a sign may not get many signs from YHWH.* (see Mattityahu 16:4).

It is important to realize that just because someone is operating with certain spiritual gifts does not mean that the person is walking in, or speaking the truth. *"The gifts and calling of Elohim are without repentance."* (Romans 11:29). The manifestation of gifts is not necessarily an affirmation of the words that exit a person's mouth. This was clearly demonstrated by Messiah when He rejected those calling Him Lord even though they claimed to be exercising gifts (Mattityahu 7:22-23).

Ultimately, I believe that the Almighty is slow to anger and thus He demonstrates His love and mercy – the

same love and mercy shown in that *"while we were yet sinners Messiah died for us."* Romans 5:8. Many long to know Him but have not been taught the full truth. He is able to discern *"the thoughts and intents of the heart."* Hebrews (Ibrim) 4:12.

We know that He is patient with us which leads to repentance (Romans 2) and that, ultimately, is the point of this discussion. He has been patient with each one of us while we have been in error. Now that you know the truth, it is up to you to repent, which means to replace wrong behavior with correct behavior. It is a humbling experience to be shown this truth - to acknowledge that you have been ignorant regarding something so simple - yet so important. This is just as much a matter of the heart as it is a matter of speech.

II

Messiah and the Name

King Dawid, in one of his many Messianic prophesies declared that Messiah would come in the Name of YHWH: "*22 The stone which the builders rejected Has become the chief cornerstone. 23 This was YHWH's doing; It is marvelous in our eyes. 24 This is the day YHWH has made; we will rejoice and be glad in it. 25 I beg O YHWH please save; O YHWH, please send prosperity. 26 Blessed is He who comes in the Name of YHWH!*" Tehillim 118:22-26.

We see this passage of Scripture fulfilled as Yahushua entered Yahrushalayim on a donkey. "*6 So the disciples went and did as Yahushua commanded them.7 They brought the donkey and the colt, laid their clothes on them, and set Him on them.8 And a very great multitude spread their clothes on the road; others cut down branches from the trees and spread them on the road.9 Then the multitudes who went before and those who followed cried out, saying: 'Hosanna to the Son of Dawid! Blessed is He who comes in the name of YHWH! Hosanna in the highest!'*" Mattityahu 21:6-9.

The crowd was clearly speaking the Name of YHWH and this is why some of the Pharisees were telling

Yahushua to rebuke His Disciples. (Luke 19:39). They had developed their own traditions and commandments called takanot (תקנת), many of which were in direct contradiction to the Torah. One of these commandments prohibited anyone other than the High Priest from uttering the Name of YHWH. To do so was considered blasphemy and a person convicted of blasphemy was subject to death by stoning. (see John (Yahanan) 10:33).

Instead of rebuking His Disciples, Yahushua responded: *"I tell you that if these should keep silent, the stones would immediately cry out."* Luke 19:40. Yahushua came in the Father's Name and it is fair to say that He spoke the Name of the Father - so He clearly would not rebuke His Disciples for following His example. The Scriptures specifically record Him stating: *"you shall by no means see me, until you say, 'Blessed is He who is coming in the Name of YHWH!'"* Mattityahu 23:39.

We can see another illustration of this fact in Mattityahu 4:4 when Yahushua quoted the Torah. The Greek translators render it as follows: *"Jesus answered, 'It is written: Man does not live on bread alone, but on every word that comes from the mouth of God.'"* Mattithyahu 4:4. He was quoting from Devarim 8:3 and the Greek manuscripts do not provide an accurate translation because Yahushua clearly would not have said "God" for reasons previously discussed and due to the fact that the word "God" does not exist in the Torah passage He was quoting.

Since He is the Living Torah, He would have quoted the Torah perfectly and the proper translation is as follows: *"Man does not live on bread alone, but by every Word that comes from the mouth of YHWH."* Devarim 8:3. It is the

Name YHWH which appears in the Torah, not the title "God." Therefore, if you believe as I do that Yahushua properly quoted the Torah, then He <u>must</u> have spoken the Name. Another example can be found in Mattityahu 22:44 where Yahushua quotes Tehillim 110:1 which states: "YHWH said to my master, '*Sit at my right hand until I make your enemies a footstool at your feet.*" Again, if Yahushua correctly quoted the Scriptures then He <u>must</u> have spoken the Name of YHWH. Also when He quoted The Shema in Mattityahu 22:37 He would have used the Name.

He affirmed this fact when He prayed: "⁶ *<u>I have manifested Your Name to the men whom You have given Me out of the world</u>. They were Yours, You gave them to Me, and they have kept Your Word.⁷ Now they have known that all things which You have given Me are from You.*" John (Yahanan) 17:6-7. He further stated: "²⁵ *O righteous Father! The world has not known You, but I have known You; and these have known that You sent Me.²⁶ And <u>I have declared to them Your Name, and will declare it</u>, that the love with which You loved Me may be in them, and I in them.*" John (Yahanan) 17:25-26.

A significant aspect of His ministry on earth was to manifest the Name of YHWH to the Elect and I believe that He was ultimately killed for speaking the Name. Many people suppose that the Pharisees sought His death simply because He claimed to be the Messiah. This is not necessarily the case, because He specifically hid that fact from most people and He instructed His Disciples not to tell anyone. (Mattityahu 16:20). There were only a handful of people to whom He actually admitted being the Messiah prior to His inquisition, such as the Samaritan woman at

the well and the man who was blind from birth. (John (Yahanan) 4:25; 9:37).

Throughout history there have been many people who have claimed to be the Messiah and were not sentenced to death. According to my understanding, the death penalty was only applicable to one claiming to be the Messiah if they were proven to be a false prophet or committed some other act worthy of death, such as blasphemy. In fact, Pilate specifically declared "*I find no fault in Him*" (Luke 23:4) immediately after Yahushua admitted that He was the Messiah.

Throughout His ministry Yahushua had been making a public spectacle of the religious leaders - the powers and principalities. He disarmed them by revealing that their traditions and man-made commands (takanot), from which they derived their authority, were of no effect. (Colossians 2:15). He had been openly proclaiming the Name of YHWH in direct contradiction to their takanot which prohibited speaking the Name. In fact, most of His actions and teachings were intentionally orchestrated to violate their takanot, while at the same time, showing His Disciples how to properly obey the Torah from their hearts.

The religious leaders accused Yahushua of many things although it appears that the charge of blasphemy was the one that ultimately resulted in the death sentence. In fact, I believe that His statement in Luke 22:66 may have decided His fate when He said: "*But from henceforth shall the Son of man be seated at the right hand of the power of YHWH.*" Many translations do not include the Name of YHWH and parallel verses in the other synoptic Gospels

fail to include this important element. There are a variety of reasons for this omission, and ample evidence exists, particularly from the Hebrew version of Mattityahu, that it was included in the original texts.

Immediately after Yahushua used the Name of YHWH we read: "⁶⁵ *Then the high priest tore his clothes, saying, 'He has spoken blasphemy! What further need do we have of witnesses? Look, now you have heard His blasphemy!* ⁶⁶ *What do you think?' They answered and said, 'He is deserving of death.'*" Mattityahu 26:65-66 NKJV. Some translations of this text describe the High Priest stating that: "*This one has cursed Elohim.*" (see Shem-Tob's Hebrew Matthew).

According to the Mishnah, the High Priest would "rent his garment" during a trial for blasphemy when the Name of YHWH was used. (Sanh., 7:5). This is exactly what we see in this text. The High Priest tore his garment and accused Yahushua of blasphemy for doing something expressly granted in the Torah, but prohibited by the takanot of the religious leaders. So we see then that the Name which gives life was likely the reason, or at least one of the reasons, for the death of the Messiah.

12

Christ

The word Christ has been attached to the name Jesus as if it were a last name ie. Jesus Christ. Christ is not a name, but rather a label which derives from pagan culture. In my opinion it carries the same negative implications as the title "lord." In fact, those who followed the Hellenistic polytheistic religious lifestyle regularly referred to their deities as lord or "kurios" (κυριος) in Greek as well as Christ, which is "christos" (χριστός) in the Greek.

It is well known that Christianity adopted certain aspects of sun god worship. The sun god Helios, whose name was inserted in place of Eliyahu in many Greek New Testament manuscripts, was called Christ (Christos) Helios and Lord (Kurios) 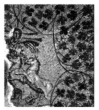 Helios the "Lord of heaven and earth." A mosaic found beneath the Vatican confirms this fact.

The Vatican was actually built atop of the Roman Pantheon, the hub of sun god worship throughout the world. Beneath this massive complex lie pagan temples and tombs, one of which was the Tomb of Julii depicting a

relief of "Christos Helios" or rather Christ Helios, the sun god riding on a chariot toward the sun. It is easy to see why they would choose his name to replace that of Eliyahu. Helios is often depicted in this fashion as can be seen from the above pictured artifact.

"Christos" is a Greek word generally defined as meaning "anointed" and it does not originate with the  Christian religion or the Christian Savior. Christos was "applied in the Greek Mysteries to a candidate who had passed the last degree and become a full initiate. Also the immanent individual god in a person, equivalent in some respects to Dionysos, Krishna, etc. What we know as Christianity is a syncretism of borrowings from Neoplatonism, neo-Pythogoreanism, Greek Gnosticism, and Hebrew religion. Christos was commonly used in the Greek translation of the Bible as a title of the Jewish Kings, those who had been anointed for reigning — a symbolic rite taken originally from the Mysteries."[70]

Concerning the word Christos: "there is little doubt that the pagans and the Christian authors of the first two centuries AD used the word synonymously with Christus, Chrestus, Christiani, and Chrestiani. According to *Realencyclopaedie*, the inscription "Chrestos" is to be seen on a Mithras relief in the Vatican. Osiris, the sun-god of Egypt, was revered as Chrestos - as was Mithra. In the Synagogue of the  Marcionites on Mount Hermon, built in the 3rd century AD, Jesus' title is spelled Chrestos, this name was used by the common people of that time. The Gnostics used the

name "Christos" as the 3rd person in their godhead — Father, Spirit (the first woman), and Son, completing the "Divine Family" - a concept adopted by Christianity."[71]

"The syncretism between Christos and Chrestos (the Sun-deity Osiris), is further elucidated by the fact of emperor Hadrian's report, who wrote, 'There are there (in Egypt) Christians who worship Serapis; and devoted to Serapis, are those  who call themselves Bishops of Christ."[72] Serapis was another Sun-deity who superseded Osiris in Alexandria. Thus it can be seen that Christ was a term applied to many pagan gods prior to the Messiah.

Many attempt to liken the term "christos" (χριστός) with the Hebrew word for anointed - mashiach (משיח), which is generally written in English as Messiah. While mashiach has been translated as "anointed" it cannot be said to be a direct translation for the word "christos." Mashiach in the general sense can refer to an anointed leader, but in the larger sense it refers to the promised deliverer of Yisra'el. Although the word mashiach is found throughout the Tanakh, and is typically translated as "anointed," on two occasions it is translated as Messiah in the English Scriptures, both in Sefer Daniel.

The Yisra'elites and Samaritans were anticipating The Mashiach (John (Yahanan) 4:20) and we read that the Disciples believed that Yahushua was The Mashiach. The Greek text even shows Andrew calling Yahushua "Messias" (Μεσσίαν) (John (Yahanan) 1:41) which would be the appropriate Greek rendering of the Hebrew word Mashiach, not Christos.

Therefore, we know that because the Greek

manuscripts were Hellenized, the word "Christ" was inserted where it otherwise should have been translated "Messiah." Just as the Name Yahushua was Hellenized as Iesous and translated into English as Jesus, so too the proper Hebrew title mashiach, was Hellenized as christos and then translated into English as Christ. Some translations have recognized this error and attempted to correct it.

"Ferrar Fenton's translation, The Complete Bible in Modern English, used "Messiah" instead of "Christ" in most places where the word is used alone, except when used as the combination "Jesus Christ." Similarly, the New English Bible has used "Messiah" in its New Testament in many places. The Good News Bible has restored the word "Messiah" in no less than 70 places in its New Testament. The New International Version gives the alternative "Messiah" in almost all places, by means of a footnote. Dr. Bullinger in The Companion Bible, appendix 98 IX, says, 'Hence, the noun (Christos) is used of and for the Messiah, and in the Gospels should always be translated "Messiah."' Also, Benjamin Wilson in his Emphatic Diaglott has restored the words "Anointed" and "Messiah" in many places."[73]

Accordingly, it does not appear appropriate to take this borrowed word from the ancient mystery religions and use it, with all of its pagan connotation, to replace the very specific word mashiach. Many pagans and polytheistic religious adherents still call their gods or spiritual leaders "christs" or "kristos." This is particularly important because the Scriptures warn of false christs or messiahs as well as the anti-christ or anti-messiah.

Even today there are many who claim to be a

Christ or "the Christ" and some are even proclaiming "the Christ" is here with us today. For many years a Christ called Lord Maitreya has been held out as the promised One. "One World, One Humanity, One Savior, One God" is the slogan used by Maitraya who allegedly is "The Lion of the Tribe of Judah, as Hebrews and Christians expect their Messiah to be: From the lineage of King David! He is also from the lineage of Prophet Muhammed (a Sayyed), as Muslims expect their Messiah to be!"⁷⁴ He provides his genealogy all the way from Adam and shows his descent from Muhammed. This Christ even comes complete with "The Great Sign" which is  littered with pagan symbolism. His teaching concerning the Great Sign allegedly describes the Seven Seals. He is presented as fulfilling prophecies from all world religions and his goal is to unite all of humanity.

Maitreya is a modern day christ and is a perfect example why I avoid this word and prefer to use Messiah or Mashiach. We were warned specifically on this point. *"For false christs and false prophets will rise and show great signs and wonders to deceive, if possible, even the elect."* Mattityahu 24:24 NKJV. When I refer to Yahushua HaMashiach there is no question that I am speaking of a Hebrew Messiah Who fulfills the prophesies provided in the Tanakh, not some New Age Christ who claims to unite all world religions.

13

Power in the Name

We read in the Scriptures that: "*The Name of YHWH is a strong tower; the righteous run to it and are safe.*" Mishle 18:10. There is strength and power in the Name of YHWH and those who belong to Him are protected by that Name. In fact, Mosheh declared in his song to the children of Yisra'el that: "*YHWH is a man of war; YHWH is His Name.*" Shemot 15:3. YHWH actually fights our battles for us and nobody understood that better than Dawid who entered into battle against the Philistine giant Goliath without any armor or conventional weapons.

Read what he stated to his enemy during the famous confrontation. "*⁴⁵ You come to me with a sword, a spear, and with a shield, but <u>I come to you in the Name of YHWH</u> of hosts, the Elohim of the ranks of Yisra'el, Whom you have defied. ⁴⁶ This day YHWH will deliver you into my hand, and I will smite you and cut off your head. And I will give the corpses of the army of the Philistines this day to the birds of the air and the wild beasts of the earth, that all the earth may know that Elohim is for Yisra'el. ⁴⁷ And all this assembly shall know that YHWH saves not with sword and spear; for the*

battle is YHWH's, and He will give you into our hands." 1 Shemuel 17:45-47.

He relied upon the Name of YHWH rather than weapons and we all know that Dawid's words came true when he sunk a stone into the giant's forehead using a slingshot. He then cut off the giant's head which sent the Philistine army fleeing. With that type of experience who better to speak of the power of the Name of YHWH. He wrote the following passage later in his life: *"¹⁰ All nations surrounded me, but <u>in the Name of YHWH I will destroy them.</u> ¹¹ They surrounded me, yes, they surrounded me; but <u>in the Name of YHWH I will destroy them.</u> ¹² They surrounded me like bees; they were quenched like a fire of thorns; for <u>in the Name of YHWH I will destroy them.</u> ¹³ You pushed me violently, that I might fall, but YHWH helped me. ¹⁴ YHWH is my strength and song, and He has become my salvation."* Tehillim 118:10-14.

Dawid knew that the Name of YHWH does not only have the power to deliver us in our battles – it also has the power to save. The Scriptures are clear that we must *"repent, and be baptized . . . in the Name of Yahushua the Messiah for the forgiveness of transgressions, and ye shall receive the gift of the Holy (Set Apart) Spirit."* Acts 2:38.⁷⁵ This issue is important because forgiveness is through the Name of Yahushua and there is power in the Name of Yahushua - which contains the Name of YHWH.

The following are some Scripture passages which reveal the importance of the Name.

- *"But as many as received him, to them gave he power to become the sons of Elohim, [even] <u>to them that believe on His Name.</u>"* John (Yahanan)⁷⁶ 1:12.
- *"Then shall they deliver you up to be afflicted, and*

shall kill you: and ye shall be hated of all nations _for My Name's sake_." Mattityahu 24:9.

- "For _where two or three are gathered together in My Name_, there am I in the midst of them." Mattityahu 18:20.

- "*13* And whatsoever ye shall ask in My Name, that will I do, that the Father may be glorified in the Son.*14* _If ye shall ask any thing in My Name, I will do [it]_." Yahanan 14:13-14.

- "_But the Comforter, [which is] the Holy (Set Apart) Spirit, whom the Father will send in My Name_, He shall teach you all things, and bring all things to your remembrance, whatsoever I have said unto you." Yahanan 14:26.

- "You have not chosen me, but I have chosen you, and ordained you, that you should go and bring forth fruit, and [that] your fruit should remain: that _whatsoever you shall ask of the Father in My Name, He may give it you_." Yahanan 15:16.

- "*20* Remember the word that I said unto you, the servant is not greater than his master. If they have persecuted me, they will also persecute you; if they have kept my saying, they will keep yours also. *21* _But all these things will they do unto you for My Name's sake_, because they know not Him that sent Me." Yahanan 15:20-21.

Yahushua performed miracles in the Name of YHWH as He stated: "_The miracles I do in my Father's Name speak for me._" Yahanan 10:25 NIV.

The story of the lame man seated at the Beautiful Gate provides a vivid example of the power of the Name.

"*1 Now Peter (Kepha)77 and Yahanan went up together to the temple at the hour of prayer, the Ninth hour.2 And a certain man lame from his mother's womb was carried, whom they laid daily at the gate of the temple which is called Beautiful, to ask alms from those who entered the temple; 3 who,*  *seeing Kepha and Yahanan about to go into the temple, asked for alms.4 And fixing his eyes on him, with Yahanan, Kepha said, 'Look at us.' 5 So he gave them his attention, expecting to receive something from them.6 Then Kepha said, 'Silver and gold I do not have, but what I do have I give you: In the Name of Mashiach Yahushua of Nazareth, rise up and walk.' 7 And he took him by the right hand and lifted him up, and immediately his feet and ankle bones received strength.8 So he, leaping up, stood and walked and entered the temple with them — walking, leaping, and praising Elohim.*" Acts 3:1-8.

The man in this story was healed in the Name of the Messiah, which contains the Father's Name. It was the Name and the man's faith in the Name which restored his body as Kepha explained to the people who gathered around. "*And His Name, through faith in His Name, has made this man strong, whom you see and know. Yes, the faith which comes through Him has given him this perfect soundness in the presence of you all.*" Acts 3:16.

Kepha and Yahanan were arrested because of the disturbance created by the healing and their subsequent teaching regarding Yahushua and His resurrection, which the Sadducees did not believe. The next day they were presented to the High Priest and some of the leaders and it is interesting to hear what they were asked. "*5 And it came*

to pass, on the next day, that their rulers, elders, and scribes, ⁶ *as well as Annas the high priest, Caiaphas, John, and Alexander, and as many as were of the family of the high priest, were gathered together at Jerusalem.* ⁷ *And when they had set them in the midst, they asked, '<u>By what power or by what Name have you done this?</u>'"* Acts 4:5-7 NKJV.

Even they recognized that there was power in a name. *"⁸ Then Kepha, filled with the Holy (Set Apart) Spirit, said to them, 'Rulers of the people and elders of Yisra'el: ⁹ If we this day are judged for a good deed done to a helpless man, by what means he has been made well, ¹⁰ let it be known to you all, and to all the people of Yisra'el, that <u>by the Name of Yahushua HaMashiach of Nazareth</u>, whom you crucified, whom Elohim raised from the dead, by Him this man stands here before you whole.¹¹ This is the 'stone which was rejected by you builders, which has become the chief stone.' ¹² Nor is there salvation in any other, for <u>there is no other Name under heaven given among men by which we must be saved</u>.'"* Acts 4:8-12. So not only is there healing by and through the Name, but salvation itself is through the Name. These seem to be some compelling reasons to get His Name right.

Now read how the religious leaders attempted to suppress the Name of Yahushua.

> *"¹³ Now when they saw the boldness of Kepha and Yahanan, and perceived that they were uneducated and untrained men, they marveled. And they realized that they had been with Yahushua.¹⁴ And seeing the man who had been healed standing with them, they could say nothing against it.¹⁵ But when they had commanded them to go aside out of the council,*

*they conferred among themselves,[16] saying,
'What shall we do to these men? For, indeed, that
a notable miracle has been done through them is
evident to all who dwell in Yahrushalayim, and
we cannot deny it.[17] But so that it spreads no
further among the people, let us severely threaten
them, that from now on they speak to no man in
this Name'   [18] So they called them and
commanded them not to speak at all nor teach in
the Name of Yahushua.[19] But Kepha and
Yahanan answered and said to them, 'Whether
it is right in the sight of Elohim to listen to you
more than to Elohim, you judge.[20] For we cannot
but speak the things which we have seen and
heard.' [21] So when they had further threatened
them, they let them go, finding no way of
punishing them, because of the people, since they
all glorified Elohim for what had been done."*
Acts 4:13-21.

The religious leaders attempted to stifle the Name
of Yahushua because there is power in the Name. This is
why the corrupt religious leaders were afraid of it and tried
to suppress it and this is why the adversary, satan, has
tried to suppress it and distort it over the centuries. It is
through belief in the Name of Yahushua that mankind
receives salvation (Yahanan 3:18). The Name itself is a
declaration that YHWH saves His people!

Salvation means life for those who are saved and
there is life in the Name. "*[30] And truly Yahushua did many
other signs in the presence of His disciples, which are not written
in this book; [31] but these are written that you may believe that*

Yahushua is HaMashiach, the Son of Elohim, and that believing you may have life in His Name." Yahanan 20:30-31.

The adversary does not want people to experience this promised life and salvation. As a result, both the Name of the Father and the Name of the Son have been suppressed, altered, replaced, polluted and corrupted, but it is the will of YHWH for His Name to be revealed and nothing can stop His will from being performed. What was said of Yisra'el in days past could be applied equally to the people of today. "*5 . . . My Name is blasphemed continually every day.[6] Therefore My people shall know My Name; therefore they shall know in that day that I am He who speaks: Behold, it is I.*'" Yeshayahu 52:5-6.

We see this desire spoken again through the Prophet Ezekiel (Yehezqel):[78] "*So I will make My Holy (Set Apart) Name known in the midst of My people Yisra'el; and I will not let them pollute My Holy (Set Apart) Name any more: and the Nations shall know that I am YHWH, the Holy (Set Apart) One of Yisra'el.*" Yehezqel 39:7.

Revealing the Name was a critical part of the work of the Messiah because there is power in the Name. Messiah walked in power as did His Disciples because they proclaimed the Name. This same power is available to all who believe in and follow Him, and this is why the Names must be restored.

14

Restoring the Names

There will come a day when YHWH will restore the pure language of Hebrew and the remnant will worship Him in unity. *"For then I will restore to the peoples a pure language, that they all may call on the Name of YHWH, to serve Him with one accord."* Zephaniyah 3:9.

Restoration involves putting things back the way they were at the beginning. In this case, the languages of the peoples will be restored to the Hebrew language which was spoken before they were confused at Babel. (Beresheet 11:9). Until that time, we need to understand that Elohim had  revealed His Name in Hebrew. As part of the necessary restoration, we need to restore the Name of Elohim, in Hebrew, which has been both suppressed and forgotten.

The Hebrew language was practically a dead language for centuries, spoken only in liturgical services in synagogues. In the past century the Hebrew language has been restored and it is now the official language of the modern State of Israel. The stage has now been set for the

restoration of the Names.

We have witnessed a time just as Amos predicted when he prophesied against Tzion and Samaria: "*And he will say, 'Hold your tongue! For we dare not mention the Name of YHWH.'*" Amos 6:10. Traditions have developed which teach, and even command, that the Name should not be spoken because it is ineffable, but nowhere is this tradition supported by Scripture. In fact, substituting the Name of YHWH with the title "LORD" or "Lord" or any other title as has been done in most modern English translations, is contrary to the commandments found within the Scriptures. "*Whatever I command you, be careful to observe it; you shall not add to it nor take away from it.*" Devarim 12:32 (also Devarim 4:2). The act of substituting the Name involves both taking away and adding.

The simple fact is that we have inherited lies as the Prophet Yirmeyahu foretold. "*19 O YHWH, my strength and my fortress, my refuge in the day of affliction, the Gentiles shall come to You from the ends of the earth and say, 'Surely our fathers have inherited lies, worthlessness and unprofitable things.' 20 Will a man make mighty ones (gods) for himself, which are not mighty ones (gods)? 21 Therefore behold, I will this once cause them to know, I will cause them to know My hand and My might; and <u>they shall know that My Name is YHWH</u>.*" Yirmeyahu 16:19-21.

Suppressing, altering or replacing the Name is clearly a violation of the First Commandment which declares: "*2 I am YHWH your Elohim, who brought you out of the land of Mitsrayim, out of the house of bondage.3 You shall have no other elohim before Me.*" Shemot 20:2-3. This command was intended to specifically identify, by Name,

the Elohim of Yisra'el. If you start substituting titles and remove the Name then you have altered the commandment and missed the point entirely.

In the Sefer Devarim, YHWH instructed the Yisra'elites when they entered the land to completely destroy the places where people worshipped false gods. YHWH specifically states: "*3 Break down their altars, smash their sacred stones and burn their Asherah poles in the fire; cut down the idols of their gods and wipe out their names from those places. 4 You must not worship YHWH your Elohim in their way. 5 But you are to seek the place YHWH your Elohim will*  *choose from among all your tribes to put his Name there for his dwelling. To that place you must go.*" Devarim 12:3-5. The goal was to abolish the names and images of the false gods and establish the Name of the One True Elohim in the Promised Land.

The notion that the Name of YHWH is suddenly ineffable or unspeakable is simply ridiculous. The Name must be remembered and it must be proclaimed according to Tehillim: "*Some trust in chariots, and some in horses; but we will remember the Name of YHWH our Elohim.*" Tehillim 20:7. We may have forgotten His Name and replaced it with the names and titles of false gods, but we have a great promise. "*20 If we had forgotten the Name of our Elohim, or stretched out our hands to a foreign god, 21 Would not Elohim search this out? For He knows the secrets of the heart.*" Tehillim 44:20-21.

Profaning the Name of YHWH was the reason why the House of Yahudah was scattered after their return

from exile. They were swearing by Baal (Lord) rather than by the Name of YHWH. "*14 Thus says YHWH concerning all My wicked neighbors who strike at the inheritance with which I have endowed My people Yisra'el, Behold I am about to uproot them from their land and will uproot the house of Yahudah from among them. 15 And it will come about that after I have uprooted them, I will again have compassion on them; and I will bring them back, each one to his inheritance and each one to his land. 16 Then if they will really learn the ways of My people, to swear by My Name, 'As YHWH lives,' even as they taught My people to swear by Baal, they will be built up in the midst of My people. 17 But if they will not listen, then I will uproot that nation, uproot and destroy it, declares YHWH.*" Yirmeyahu 12:14-17.79*

Despite being scattered around the world, YHWH has promised to restore the House of Yisra'el <u>for the sake of His Name</u>!

"*16 Again the Word of YHWH came to me: 17 Son of man, when the people of Yisra'el were living in their own land, they defiled it by their conduct and their actions. Their conduct was like a woman's monthly uncleanness in my sight. 18 So I poured out my wrath on them because they had shed blood in the land and because they had defiled it with their idols. 19 I dispersed them among the nations, and they were scattered through the countries; I judged them according to their conduct and their actions. 20 And wherever they went among the nations they profaned My set apart Name, for it was said of them, 'These are the YHWH's people, and yet they had to*

leave his land.' ²¹ <u>*I had concern for My set apart*</u> <u>*Name, which the house of Yisra'el profaned*</u> <u>*among the nations where they had gone.*</u> ²² *Therefore say to the house of Yisra'el, 'This is what the Sovereign YHWH says: It is not for your sake, O house of Yisra'el, that* <u>*I am going*</u> <u>*to do these things, but for the sake of My set*</u> <u>*apart Name,*</u> *which you have profaned among the nations where you have gone.* ²³ *I will set apart My Great Name, which has been profaned among the Gentiles, the Name you have profaned among them. Then the Gentiles will know that I am YHWH, declares the Master YHWH, when I show Myself set apart through you before their eyes."* Yehezqel 36:16-23.

The Hebrew word for profane is halal (חלל) which means "to hollow out," "to dissolve" also "to pierce" and "to wound." According to Yeshayahu 53:5 the Messiah was "wounded" or "pierced" (halal) for our transgressions. As the Name was profaned so too was the Messiah profaned. As a result of the profaning and for the sake of the Name, YHWH provided a wonderful promise of a Renewed Covenant where He would: "²⁴ *. . . take you from among the nations, gather you out of all countries, and bring you into your own land.²⁵ Then I will sprinkle clean water on you, and you shall be clean; I will cleanse you from all your filthiness and from all your idols.²⁶ I will give you a new heart and put a new spirit within you; I will take the heart of stone out of your flesh and give you a heart of flesh.²⁷* <u>*I will put My Spirit within you and*</u> <u>*cause you to walk in My statutes, and you will keep My*</u> <u>*judgments and do them."*</u> Yehezqel 36:24-28. This is the work

of the Messiah for the sake of the Name!

The Scriptures are full of examples of the importance and meaning of names. All of the Prophets had names which had meaning and significance. As with the Names of the Father and Son, translators have chosen to change and, at times, "Hellenize"[80] the names of certain patriarchs.

The name of the prophet Isaiah is spelled ישעיהו in Hebrew and is pronounced Yesha Yahu. Yeshayahu like Yahushua means: "YHWH saves" or "YHWH is salvation" or "salvation of YHWH." It is interesting that this name has the same meaning as the Name Yahushua. The prophesies in the Scroll of Yeshayahu speak considerably about the Messiah and the oldest Scroll of Yeshayahu was found completely intact this century in a cave near Qumran which is located next to the Dead Sea. It is currently on display in The Shrine of the Book at the Israel Museum in Jerusalem. It is no coincidence that The Scroll of Yeshayahu is at center stage during this day and age when many anticipate the return of Messiah. The Messianic prophesies are on display for all to read in the Hebrew language.

Some other examples of Names which have been changed are: Jeremiah which is spelled ירמיהו and more accurately pronounced Yirme <u>Yahu</u>. The name means "exalted of YHWH" or "appointed of YHWH." The name of the prophet Zechariah means "Yah is remembered" or "Yah is renowned" and is spelled זכריה in Hebrew and pronounced Zakar <u>Yah</u>. Matthew in Hebrew

is מתתיהו more accurately transliterated Mattit Yahu because the name means "gift of YHWH."

These are only a sample of the names of our predecessors in the faith which have been altered to the point that they are not pronounced correctly. Notice that in all of these instances, the Name of Yah has been removed. You have heard about something being lost in the translation. Well much is lost in transliteration when the original name of a prophet, an individual, the Messiah or the Almighty is not used.

It was prophesied that the Name would be polluted, but then it would be known in the midst of Yisra'el and by the heathen (ie. the Goyim, the Nations, the Gentiles). "*So I will make My Set Apart Name known in the midst of My people Yisra'el; and I will not let them pollute My Set Apart Name any more: and the heathen shall know that I am YHWH, the Set Apart One of Yisra'el.*" Yehezqel 39:7. We are seeing this prophecy come to pass in this generation.

Not only will the Nations know the Name, but YHWH will take out from the Gentiles a people *for His Name.* "*[13] And after they had become silent, James (Ya'akov) answered, saying, Men and brethren, listen to me: [14] Simon has declared how Elohim at the first visited the Gentiles to take out of them a people for His Name. [15] And with this the words of the prophets agree, just as it is written: [16] 'After this I will return and will rebuild the tabernacle of Dawid, which has fallen down; I will rebuild its ruins, and I will set it up; [17] So that the rest of mankind may seek YHWH, even all the Gentiles who are called by My Name, says YHWH who does all these things.' [18] Known to Elohim from eternity are all His works.*" Acts 15:13-18.

Those who love the Name will be brought to the set

apart mountain of YHWH to serve and rejoice.

> "*1 Thus says YHWH: 'Keep justice, and do righteousness, for My salvation is about to come, and My righteousness to be revealed. 2 Blessed is the man who does this, and the son of man who lays hold on it; who keeps from defiling the Sabbath, and keeps his hand from doing any evil. 3 Do not let the son of the foreigner who has joined himself to YHWH Speak, saying, 'YHWH has utterly separated me from His people'; nor let the eunuch say, 'Here I am, a dry tree.' 4 For thus says YHWH: 'To the eunuchs who keep My Sabbaths, and choose what pleases Me, and hold fast My covenant, 5 Even to them I will give in My house and within My walls a place and a name better than that of sons and daughters; I will give them an everlasting name that shall not be cut off. 6 Also the sons of the foreigner (Gentiles) who join themselves to YHWH, to serve Him, <u>and to love the Name of YHWH,</u> to be His servants, all who guard the Sabbath, and not profane it, and hold fast my covenant − 7them I shall bring to My set-apart mountain, and let them rejoice in My house of prayer. Their burnt offerings and their slaughterings are accepted on My altar, for My house is called a house of prayer for all peoples.'"*

Yeshayahu 56:1-7.

What a fabulous promise for Gentiles who join themselves to YHWH, who love His Name, who keep the Sabbaths and hold fast to His covenant.

Restoring the true Name in our worship is one of the primary aspects of restoration which is now occurring within the Assembly of Believers – Yisra'el. YHWH wants His people to be praising His Name, not the name of some pagan idol or some abstract, non-descript title. This could not be made any clearer as He declares: *"I Am YHWH, that is My Name, and My glory (esteem) I do not give to another, nor My praise to idols."* Yeshayahu 42:8. Again in Yeshayahu we read: *"For your Maker is your Husband - YHWH Almighty is His Name - the Holy (Set Apart) One of Yisra'el is your Redeemer; He is called the Elohim of all the earth."* Yeshayahu 54:5.

His Name is important. Those who love YHWH will recognize that fact: they will love His Name and they will worship His Name and He will reward those who know and worship His Name. *"14 Because he has set his love upon Me, therefore I will deliver him; <u>I will set him on high, because he has known My Name.</u> 15 He shall call upon Me, and I will answer him; I will be with him in trouble; I will deliver him and honor him. 16 With long life I will satisfy him, and show him My salvation."* Tehillim 91:14-16.

It is my hope that the reader can clearly see the grievous error which has occurred over the centuries resulting in the suppression of the True Name of YHWH and the Messiah, along with a substitution of either meaningless or pagan names. I urge every reader to prayerfully consider the Names and begin using them. At the same time we all need to pray that our tongues would be purified and cleansed from any defilement which has occurred from the past use of such abominable names. From this point on, it should be determined that the names

of any false gods will not pass through your lips. "*And in all that I have said to you, be circumspect and make no mention of the name of other gods, nor let it be heard from your mouth.*" Shemot 23:13 NKJV.

The reason that YHWH brought the children of Yisra'el out of Mitsrayim in such a dramatic fashion was so His Name would be revealed throughout all the world. Read what Mosheh was to tell Pharaoh on behalf of YHWH: "*But indeed for this purpose I have raised you up, that I may show My power in you, and that My Name may be declared in all the earth.*" Shemot 9:16 NKJV. The word "declared' means to be announced openly or spoken. Therefore the tradition of men which teaches not to speak the Name is completely contrary to the desire of YHWH for the entire world to know His Name.

It would appear from this passage, and many others, that one of the primary functions of Yisra'el was to reveal the Name of YHWH to the world. If modern day Judaism is doing the exact opposite by prohibiting the use of the Name, then they are not operating in accordance with the mission of Yisra'el, the Set Apart Assembly of YHWH. The same holds true for the Christian religion.

The ministry of Yahushua was centered around bringing esteem to the Name of YHWH. "*27 Now My soul is troubled, and what shall I say? Father, save Me from this hour? But for this purpose I came to this hour.*28 *Father, <u>glorify Your Name</u>. Then a voice came from heaven, saying, '<u>I have both glorified it and will glorify it again</u>.*'" Yahanan 12:27-28.

I know for certain that I have been commanded to speak, declare, magnify, shout and praise the Name of YHWH. I also know for certain that His Name is not

GOD, the LORD, Adonai, HaShem or Jehovah. Therefore why would I replace His Name with a title or name that I know is wrong? It simply does not make any sense.

We have forgotten the Name but that does not mean that we cannot remember it. If we refuse to prayerfully seek out His True Name and resign ourselves to using false names or titles then we should not expect to ever learn the truth. I believe that we all need to take a step of faith and begin to utter the Name prayerfully and reverently. As we continue, the Ruach (Spirit) will guide our tongues in truth. After all the Spirit has been sent in the Name of Yahushua. *"But the Helper, the Ruach Hakodesh, whom <u>the Father will send in My Name</u>, He will teach you all things, and bring to your remembrance all things that I said to you."* Yahanan 14:26.

Once we have been taught by the Ruach then we will be able to praise as King Dawid. *"¹ Praise YHWH! (Hallelu Yah!) Praise, O servants of YHWH, praise the Name of YHWH! ² Blessed be the Name of YHWH from this time forth and forever ³ <u>from the rising of the sun to the going down of it and from east to west, the Name of YHWH is to be praised</u>!"* Tehillim 113:1-3.

15

In the End

There is currently a trend in the Messianic world which avoids and sometimes forbids using the Name of YHWH so as not to offend the Jews (the Yahudim). I agree that it is important not to intentionally offend others. I also agree that we should honor many of the proper traditions preserved and observed by the Yahudim. That having been said, I do not believe that we should neglect a command so as not to offend those who have decided to avoid or suppress the Name, no matter what their motivation or intention.

I would bet that if a Christian asked a Jew not to wear a tallit, tzit tzit or tefellin[81] because they found it offensive, the Jew would probably respectfully tell the Christian where they could go - and rightly so. Just because the Christian might believe  that the Torah was abolished does not mean that the Jew should stop observing the Torah out of respect for the Christian.

Likewise, I would not expect anyone to avoid using

the Name, which is a commandment, because another incorrectly finds it offensive. It is their thinking and conduct which needs to be corrected, not the one using the Name reverently. Once you find the truth it is important that you walk in it, otherwise you really do not hold the truth.[82]

In every case you need to use wisdom and I would encourage everyone to always act in love. In the end, we need to place our focus on YHWH and set things straight with Him before we worry about men and all of their customs, traditions and idiosyncrasies.

As a final point of reflection, the life and ministry of Paul (Shaul)[83] revolved around the Name of the Messiah. Prior to his conversion Shaul first persecuted people for calling on the Name of Yahushua as he stated "*I too was convinced that I ought to do all that was possible to oppose the name of Yahshua of Nazareth.*" Acts 26:9. You see, the Name of Yahushua was not just a moniker, it represented His teachings, His nature, His will and His desires. Shaul opposed the Name because it represented a threat to his authority and much of what he had been taught as a Pharisee.

After his powerful conversion on the road to Damascus, Shaul was called to bear the Name of Yahushua to the world. Read the vision that Yahushua gave to Ananias (Hananyah): "*[13] Then Hananyah answered, 'Master, I have heard from many about this man, how much harm he has done to Your set apart ones in Yahrushalayim. [14] And here he has authority from the chief priests to bind all who call on Your*

Name.' ¹⁵ But the Master said to him, 'Go, for <u>he is a chosen vessel of Mine to bear My Name before Gentiles, kings, and the children of Yisra'el.</u> ¹⁶ For I will show him how many things <u>he must suffer for My Name's sake.</u>'" Acts 9:13-16.

The ministry of Shaul was to bear the Name of Yahushua to the Gentiles, kings and the children of Yisra'el and it appears that the central ministry of all of the Disciples was to advance the Name. *"It was for the sake of the Name that they went out, receiving no help from the pagans."* 3 Yahanan 7.

The ultimate goal of this study is to present how important names are to the Almighty, not only in the past, but also in the future. The Scriptures describe the faithful Assembly as *those who have kept His word and have not denied His Name.* (Revelation 3:8). There is also the promise that those who overcome *will be given a new name* and *the Name of YHWH will be written on them.* (Revelation 2:17; 3:12). All of the servants of YHWH are sealed with His Name. *"3 The throne of Elohim and of the Lamb will be in the city, and his servants will serve Him. 4 They will see His face, and His Name will be on their foreheads."* Revelation 22:3-4. The 144,000 who will stand on Mount Tzion with the Lamb, will have the *"Father's Name written on their foreheads"* Revelation 14:1-2 (some texts read *"the Lamb's Name and His Father's Name"*).

The following is the Aaronic Priestly blessing which was spoken over the children of Yisra'el in order to actually place the Name of YHWH upon them: *"24 YHWH bless you and keep you; 25 YHWH make His face shine upon you, and be gracious to you; 26 YHWH lift up His countenance upon you, and give you peace."* Bemidbar 6:24-26.

As was mentioned at the beginning of this book, the Hebrew word shem (שם) besides meaning "name" can also mean "mark." Thus, being sealed with a name is, in essence, the same as receiving a mark. (see Revelation 13:17).

As we have studied the issue of the Name of Elohim we have witnessed a vivid example of how 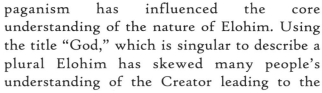 paganism has influenced the core understanding of the nature of Elohim. Using the title "God," which is singular to describe a plural Elohim has skewed many people's understanding of the Creator leading to the diminishment of the Name and the adoption of pagan trinities which emanate from Gentile cultures.[84] Christianity has divided Elohim, into three distinct persons, when He clearly declares that He is One and His Name is One. (Devarim 6:4). I remember singing the verse "God in three persons blessed trinity" never realizing that this was a man-made concept completely unsupported by the Scriptures. We need to get the Name right so that we can properly understand the nature of Elohim.

It is my desire that people understand the true nature of the Elohim of Yisra'el and that those who profess to believe in Him begin using the Names of YHWH and Yahushua in their prayers and worship. In order to worship Elohim in Spirit and in Truth, we must use the true Names so that we can pray as King Dawid did when he declared:

*"I will bow down toward your Holy Temple and will praise
Your Name for Your love and Your faithfulness, for You have
exalted above all things
Your Name and Your Word."*[85]

. . . The Father and The Son.

Endnotes

1   The term "Old Testament" is often used to describe the Scriptures commonly known as the "Jewish Bible" or the Tanakh (see endnote 30). I believe that the term is terribly misleading because it gives the impression that everything contained therein is old or outdated. While growing up in a mainline Christian denomination I was given the distinct impression that it was full of great stories, but it applied to "The Jews" and was ultimately replaced by the "New Testament" which contained the important Scriptures for Christians. While this may or may not have been done intentionally, I believe that it is a notion which is pervasive throughout much of the Christian religion. Without a doubt, the Tanakh and in particular, the Torah (see endnote 28) are essential to the faith and these are the Scriptures which must be at the core of every person's belief system. If these truths are not at the foundation and considered completely relevant for today, then people are prone to be misled and follow false and twisted doctrines. This matter is discussed at length in The Walk in the Light series book entitled "Scriptures."

2   Beresheet is the transliteration of the Hebrew word בראשית which is often translated as Genesis. It means "in the beginning" and it is the name of the first book found in the Scriptures as well as the first word in that book. Keep in mind that I use the word "book" very loosely because in this modern day we use books in codex form which are bound by a spine and generally have writing on both pages. By using the word "book" we create a mental image regarding manuscripts which may not be accurate. Manuscripts such as the Torah (see endnote 28) and other writings in the Tanakh (see endnote 30) were written on scrolls, so instead of the word book, it is more accurate to refer to the scroll or the sefer

(ספר) when referring to these ancient manuscripts. Therefore the "book" of Beresheet would be more accurately described as Sefer Beresheet ספר בראשית since it originally came as a scroll.

3   The problems which are found in many English translations is a topic of the Walk in the Light series book entitled "Scriptures." It is important to make the distinction between the inerrancy of the Word and the inerrancy of a particular translation. In the present context I am only referring to errors made by human translators to the written word verses the inerrant Living Word.

4   You will find that the words "Jewish,""Jews" and "Jew" are in italics because they are ambiguous and sometimes derogatory terms. At times these expressions are used to describe all of the genetic descendants of Jacob (Ya'akov) while at other times the words describe adherents to the religion called Judaism. The terms are commonly applied to ancient Yisra'elites as well as modern day descendents of those tribes, whether they are atheists or Believers in the Almighty. The word "Jew" originally referred to a member of the tribe of Judah (Yahudah) or a person that lived in the region of Judea. After the different exiles of the House of Yisra'el and the House of Yahudah, it was the Yahudim that returned to the land while the House of Yisra'el was scattered to the ends of the earth (Yirmeyahu 9:16). Since the Yahudim were the recognizable descendents of Ya'akov, over time with the Kingdom of Yisra'el in exile, the Yahudim came to represent Yisra'el and thus the term "Jew" came to represent a Yisra'elite. While this label became common and customary, it is not accurate and is the cause of tremendous confusion. This subject is described in greater detail in the Walk in the Light Series book entitled "The Redeemed."

5   The term "heathen" is generally used to refer to one who does not believe in and obey the Creator of the Universe as described in the Hebrew Scriptures. It is actually synonymous with the word "Gentile" or goy which would refer to the nations other than Yisra'el. In this book I will use

this term loosely and often interchangeably with the word pagan. Although these words can be used in a derogatory fashion, that is not my intent. Rather, the words are used to help identify those people who worship false gods as a whole, unless otherwise noted.

6   American Heritage Dictionary.

7   Webster's New World Dictionary.

8   Syncretism is a technical word which simply means "merging." It describes the process of merging two religions together and was used quite often by the Catholic Church when attempting to "convert" heathens. It was determined that allowing the converts to maintain some of their traditions made the conversion process more palatable. This was actually done by the Roman Emperor Constantine when he originally established the Roman Catholic Church. Being an avid sun god worshipper himself, he mixed aspects of sun worship and the faith of the Believers in the Messiah which resulted in a new religion combining elements of both. The mixing continued over the centuries by adding pagan beliefs and practices to the point where both modern Protestant Christianity as well as the Catholic Churches (Eastern and Roman) are nothing like the faith practiced and preached by the original Disciples and Believers in the Messiah.

9   *Come Out of Her My People*, C.J. Koster, Institute For Scripture Research, (2001) Page 53.

10 Keil & Delitzsch Commentary on the Old Testament: New Updated Edition, Electronic Database. Copyright (c) 1996 by Hendrickson Publishers, Inc.

11 The word pagan is used in the most general sense to describe all false religions and beliefs that worship idols, deities and/or concepts which are contrary to the truth found within the Hebrew Scriptures commonly called the "Old Testament" and the Messianic Scriptures commonly called the "New Testament." The subject of paganism, its origins, development and infiltration into modern society is discussed in detail in the Walk in the Light series book entitled "Restoration."

12   I have heard it argued that since Gad is actually the name of one of the Twelve Tribes of Yisra'el then "God" must be acceptable. We are talking apples and oranges here. No one ever worshipped Gad or the Tribe of Gad as the Creator. On the other hand Baal-Gad or Baal-God which literally means "Lord God" was historically in direct competition for worship with the Creator. That being the case I think that it would be wise to steer away from anything that even has the appearance of impropriety. There are better, more accurate and more Scriptural titles to use. Granted I will use this terminology when I am trying to get a point across to someone who is not familiar with any other term, but in my worship and fellowship I like to avoid improper terms. It is a good habit to get into if you plan on spending eternity with the Creator.

13   Deuteronomy (Devarim) 6:4 has always been one of the most important prayers to Yisra'el known as the Shema or Sh'ma. It describes the Creator as being One or "the One and Only" which flies in the face of the Christian doctrine of the Trinity. All Christians are familiar with the chorus "God in three persons blessed trinity." The concept of the trinity derives from pagan doctrines and is discussed further in the Walk in the Light series book entitled "Restoration."

14   Zekaryah (זכריה) is the proper Hebrew transliteration for the name of the Prophet often called Zechariah.

15   The word "Bible" is placed in quotes because while it has been traditionally used to describe the collection of documents considered by Christianity to be inspired by Elohim, I prefer the use of the word Scriptures. The word Bible derives from Byblos which has more pagan connotations than I prefer, especially when referring to the written Word of Elohim. This subject is discussed in greater detail in the Walk in the Light Series book entitled "Scriptures."

16   *The Dictionary of the Bible*, McKenzie, 1977, Page 72.

17   McClintock and Strong Encyclopedia, Electronic Database, Copyright 2000 by Biblesoft.

18   Yisra'el is the English transliteration for the Hebrew word
      יִשְׂרָאֵל often spelled Israel.

19   Yirmeyahu (יִרְמִיָהוּ) is the proper transliteration for the
      Hebrew name of the prophet commonly called Jeremiah.

20   The synagogue was not always a place exclusively for
      adherents to the religion of Judaism. Rather it was a place
      where Yisra'elites would gather to assemble and study. The
      early followers of the Messiah, who were mostly Yisra'elites
      continued to assemble in the synagogues when not in
      Jerusalem (Yahrushalayim). Eventually, after the destruction
      of the Temple, the Pharisaic sect took over the reigns of the
      religious life of Yisra'elites. The followers of the Messiah
      who would not submit to the authority of the Pharisees
      eventually stopped assembling with them. Now the
      synagogue is something exclusively used by adherents of
      Judaism which represents the descendents of the Pharisees.
      "The Orthodox and Chasidim typically use the word "shul,"
      which is Yiddish. The word is derived from a German word
      meaning "school," and emphasizes the synagogue's role as a
      place of study. Conservative Jews usually use the word
      "synagogue," which is actually a Greek translation of Beit
      K'nesset and means "place of assembly" (it's related to the
      word "synod"). Reform Jews use the word "temple," because
      they consider every one of their meeting places to be
      equivalent to, or a replacement for, The Temple."
      www.shomairyisrael.org.

21   The word "church" is a man-made word generally associated
      with the Catholic and Christian religions. In that context it is
      typically meant to describe the corporate body of faith but it
      can also be used to describe a building. It is used in most
      modern English Bibles as a translation for the Greek word
      ekklesia (εκκλεσια) which simply means the "called out
      assembly of YHWH." The word "church" derives from
      pagan origins and its misuse is part of the problem associated
      with Replacement Theology which teaches that the "Church"
      has replaced Yisra'el, which in Hebrew is called the qahal
      (קהל): "the called out assembly of YHWH." The Hebrew

"qahal" and Greek "ekklesia" are the same thing: The Commonwealth of Yisra'el. Therefore, the continued use of the word "church" is divisive and confusing. This subject is described in greater detail in the Walk in the Light series book entitled "The Redeemed."

22 The Sefer Malachi goes into detail how His people and particularly the priests profaned His worship by despising His Name and presenting defective offerings. (see Malachi 1:6-14).

23 www.krishna.com

24 El Shaddai (אל שדי) is the Hebrew Name which is translated Elohim Almighty.

25 A bondservant is the relationship which exists when an individual decides to follow Elohim. The Scriptures depict a person who was a slave or servant and entitled to their freedom in the seventh (Sabbath) year, but because of the love that they have for their Master they willingly submit to serve Him and become a part of His household <u>forever</u>. (Shemot 21:1-6). Many of the early disciples described themselves as bondservants including Shaul and Timotheos (Philippians 1:1; Titus 1:1, Romans 1:1), Epaphras (Colossians 4:12), Ya'akov (Ya'akov 1:1), Shimon Kepha (2 Kepha 1:1) and Yahudah (Yahudah 1). Even the Messiah was described as taking the form of a Bondservant (Philippians 2:7).

26 Contrary to popular belief, the modern Christian religion is not the same faith as that which was practiced by the first Disciples of the Messiah and Yisra'el. All of the original Disciples were Yisra'elites and all of the original Believers were Yisra'elites. Early Gentile converts were "grafted in" to the Olive Tree which represents The Commonwealth of Yisra'el (Romans 11). Over the decades and centuries that followed the death and resurrection of Messiah, pagan doctrines and anti-Semitism infiltrated and divided the Assembly of Believers. The historical persecution of the Yisra'elites by the Roman Empire led to the demise of the Yisra'elite Believers (commonly called Nazoreans) and the surge of Christianity, which perpetrated the concept that "The Church" had replaced the Elect of Elohim, which is

Yisra'el. The Christian Religion through the Catholic Church was officially established by the Roman Empire in the Third Century C.E. and by that time there had been a significant departure from the original faith presented in the Scriptures by Abraham (Abraham), Isaac (Yitshaq), Jacob (Ya'akov), Moses (Mosheh), the Prophets and the Messiah (Mashiach). The new religion called Christianity was a mixture of the truth, anti-Semitism and sun god worship which has twisted and distorted Scriptures for centuries to become a religion of lawlessness that stands diametrically opposed to the will and commandments of Elohim. This issue is discussed in greater detail in the Walk in the Light series book entitled "Law and Grace."

Contrary to popular belief, Rabbinic Judaism is not the same religion as that of the Yisra'el which we read about in the Scriptures. Rabbinic Judaism is a religion which was developed largely because of the Great Revolt. After the siege on Jerusalem (Yahrushalayim) and the destruction of the Second Temple by Titus in 70 A.D., the Pharisees and possibly the only surviving Sanhedrin member Yahanan ben Zakkai founded an Academy at Yavneh which became the center of Rabbinic Authority. His predecessor Gamaliel II continued to solidify the power base of the Pharisaic Sect of the Hebrews who, through their cooperation with the Roman Empire, were able to survive the near annihilation which was suffered by the other Yisra'elite sects such as the Sadducees, the Essenes, the Zealots, the Sicarii and the Nazoreans. There were still other sects of Yisra'elites about which history provides scant detail such as the Therapeutae and those who composed the "Odes of Solomon." In any event, the Pharisees, through the enhancement of Rabbinic authority and the leadership of Rabbi Akiba developed into the leading Yisra'elite sect which is now known as Rabbinic Judaism. While Rabbinic Judaism claims to stem directly from Yisra'el it is not much different from the Roman Catholic church claiming a direct line of "Popes" to Simon Peter (Shimon Kepha). These claims of authority are quite meaningless as neither religious system

represents the pure faith found in the Scriptures. Rabbinic Judaism, while it may consist of mostly genetic descendents of Abraham, Yitshaq and Ya'akov, is not Yisra'el. In other words, you do not have to convert to Judaism to become part of the Commonwealth of Yisra'el (ie. the Kingdom of Elohim) nor do you have to accept Talmudic teaching to follow Elohim or submit to Rabbinic authority. Rabbinic Judaism does not have a Temple nor a priesthood and their Rabbinic power structure is not supported or condoned by the Scriptures. This is why the Talmud, which is not Scripture, is so important in Rabbinic Judaism, because it lends credence to their newly devised system. When the Messiah returns He will set things straight. He will find and lead His sheep and He will not need any Catholic priests, Christian Pastors or Jewish Rabbis to help Him.

28   The Torah (תורה) consists of the first five books of the Hebrew and Christian Scriptures. They were written by Moses (Mosheh) and collectively they are often referred to as "The Law" in many modern English translations of the Scriptures. The Torah is more accurately defined as the "instruction" of Elohim for His set apart people. The Torah contains instruction for those who desire to live righteous, set apart lives in accordance with the will of Elohim. The names of the five different "books" are transliterated from their proper Hebrew names as follows: Genesis – Beresheet, Exodus – Shemot, Leviticus – Vayiqra, Numbers – Bemidbar, Deuteronomy – Devarim.

29   Egypt is the modern word used to describe the land inhabited by the descendents of Mitsrayim, who was the son of Ham (Beresheet 10:6). Thus, throughout this text the word Mitsrayim will be used in place of the English word Egypt since that is how it is rendered in the Torah.

30   The Tanakh is the compilation of Scriptures commonly referred to as The Hebrew Bible or The Old Testament in Christian Bibles. It consists of the Torah (Instruction), Nebi'im (Prophets) and the Kethubim (Writings), thus the

Hebrew acronym TNK which is pronounced tah-nak.

31 The Sefer Hoshea gives an excellent example of how names are used by Elohim to demonstrate His purpose and plan. Hoshea was commanded to marry Gomer, a harlot. They had three children together named Jezreel, Lo-Ruhamah and Lo Ammi. Jezreel is Yisre'el (יזרעאל) in Hebrew and means "El scatters" or "El sows." Lo-Ruhamah (לא רחמה) means "no mercy" and Lo-Ammi (לא עמי) means "not my people." Therefore, El was teaching that He would scatter the House of Yisra'el, that He would not have mercy upon them, that they would then not be considered His people any longer and He would not be considered their Elohim. The prophesy does not stop there because He states that their numbers would be as the sand of the sea, a promise given to Abraham and Ya'akov. He then states that they would be gathered together with the House of Yahudah (Hoshea 1:11). This regathering is a prophesied event which has yet to occur. The marriage and subsequent redemption of Gomer is critical to understanding this prophesy. Hoshea, which means "salvation" is a clear reference to the Messiah. He married a prostitute, which represents the House of Yisra'el. Instead of remaining true to her Husband she continues to prostitute herself. Hoshea later redeems (purchases) her for a price (15 shekels of silver and one and one half omer of barley). This is symbolic of the redemption that the Messiah has paid for His Bride.

32 Canonization is a man-made concept which determines whether certain writings are included within the accepted Scriptures. The canonization of the modern day Bible took place at the Council of Laodicea in Phrygia Pacatiana somewhere between 343 A.D and 381 A.D. A commonly accepted date is 364 A.D. although no one can say for certain when the Synod took place. This subject is addressed in detail in the Walk in the Light series book entitled "Scriptures."

33 Mishle (משלי) is the proper transliteration for the Hebrew word which is commonly called Proverbs.

34 Mosheh is the proper transliteration for the name of the Patriarch commonly called Moses.

35   *Introductory Hebrew Grammar*, R. Laird Harris, p. 16.

36   *Fossilized Customs*, Lew White, Strawberry Islands Publishers, Fourth Printing (2002) Page 16.

37   *Old Testament Textual Criticism*, Ellis R. Brotzman, Baker Book House 1999.

38   *The Scriptures*, Institute for Scripture Research, 1998, p. xii.

39   Yitshaq is a proper transliteration for the Hebrew Patriarch commonly called Isaac.

40   Ribkah is a proper transliteration for the Hebrew Matriarch commonly called Rebecca.

41   Ya'akov is a proper transliteration for the Hebrew Patriarch commonly called Jacob.

42   Revelation 1:8, 21:6 and 22:13 provide a critical key to this mystery of the Aleph Taw (את). While Greek translations of these texts have the Messiah saying: "I am the Alpha (A) and the Omega (Ω)" it is quite apparent that this Hebrew Messiah was speaking to His Hebrew Disciple in Hebrew or Aramaic. Therefore Yahushua would have declared: "I am the Aleph (א) and the Taw (ת)." The Messiah is the Aleph Taw (את) which is imbedded throughout the Tanakh, and particularly the Torah. Therefore, when you read the Hebrew Scriptures you will find the Messiah embedded throughout the pages, often times un-translated but at critical points. The Targums also provide a translation from the Aramaic which describe "The Memra" which is translated into the English as "The Word." The Memra is another vivid example of the Messiah in the Scriptures which is often overlooked in modern English translations.

43   Ibrim is a proper transliteration for the word Hebrews.

44   Dawid is the correct transliteration for the King of Yisra'el commonly called David. The name is spelled דוד or דויד in Hebrew. It is well understood that the vav (ו) had a "w" sound in ancient Hebrew thus "Dawid" which means "beloved".

45   Tehillim (תהלים) is a proper transliteration for the word Psalms. The Book of Psalms would thus be rendered Sefer Tehillim.

46   *The Chumash*, The Stone Edition, Mesorah Publications Ltd, 2000, p. 319.

47   See Endnote 42.

48   Some might believe that the Messiah negated or altered this command due to the passage in Mattityahu 5:34-36 but further review of the Aramaic text reveals that He was speaking of swearing falsely, not swearing in the Name of YHWH. In fact, in a prophesy given by Yirmeyahu, YHWH stated: "*15 But after I uproot them, I will again have compassion and will bring each of them back to his own inheritance and his own country. 16 And if they learn well the ways of my people and swear by My Name, saying, 'As surely as YHWH lives' - even as they once taught my people to swear by Baal - then they will be established among my people. 17 But if any nation does not listen, I will completely uproot and destroy it*," declares YHWH." Yirmeyahu 12:15-17. This appears to be the reason for the destruction of the Temple, more accurately called The House of YHWH.

49   The collection of writings commonly called "The New Testament" is better called The Messianic Scriptures because they describe the past and future work of the Messiah. The New Covenant, more accurately called the Renewed Covenant is found in the Tanakh, which is just as relevant today as the Messianic Scriptures. They fit together as a complete package and the "New" does not replace or supersede the "Old." In fact, early Believers only had the Tanakh as the Messianic Scriptures were not written for decades after the resurrection of the Messiah. I believe that the Torah is the foundation for faith in YHWH and therefore I avoid using the "Old" and "New" distinctions which tend to diminish the significance of the Tanakh. This subject is described in greater detail in the Walk in the Light Series books entitled "Scriptures" and "Covenants."

50   Yahushua (יהושע) is the proper transliteration for the Hebrew name often called Joshua in English.

51   We must always be in the habit of testing things according to the Tanakh, just as the Bereans did in Acts 17:11. They searched the Tanakh and believed as a result of what they read. This is how we must support our belief, with proof from

the Tanakh and if you read or hear anything that contradicts the Tanakh then it must be treated as false.

52 Melchizedek (מלכי־צדק) is a Hebrew word which is really the combination of two Hebrew words namely: "King" which is melek (מלך) and "Righteous" which is tsedeq (צדק). The Scriptures describe Melchizedek as the King of Salem (Peace), the Priest (Cohen) of the El Most High. (Beresheet 14:18). In a clear Messianic prophesy Dawid declares: *"You are a priest forever according to the order of Melchizedek."* Tehillim 110:4. The Sefer Hebrews, better known as Ibrim, later describes how the Messiah is our High Priest according to the order of Melchizedek, not the order of Levi. (Ibrim 7). It is critical to understand how the Messiah functions as High Priest and Melchizedek is the key.

53 The crossing of the River was a symbolic immersion commonly called Baptism within Christianity. This was a ritual cleansing just as occurred when Mosheh lead Yisra'el through the parted sea.

54 We know that the Messiah would circumcise our hearts.

55 We are told that the Messiah will conquer the world and rule from Mt. Tzion.

56 Barnes' notes: (Note on Matthew 1:21). In this quote the word "Yisra'elites" has been inserted in place of the word "Jews." This was done for clarity and consistency. For a more detailed discussion of these terms refer to footnote 4.

57 *The Acts of the Apostles*, by Jackson and Lake.

58 *Smith's Bible Dictionary.*

59 A dictionary of the Bible, by James Hastings.

60 Alford's Greek New Testament, An Exegetical and Critical Commentary.

61 Encyclopedia Americana (Vol.16, p. 41).

62 Encyclopedia Britannica (15th ed. Vol. 10 p.149).

63 Fausset's Bible Dictionary, Electronic Database Copyright (c) 1998 by Biblesoft.

64 Mattityahu (מתתיהו) is the proper transliteration of the Hebrew name which is often spelled Matthew in English. The name contains the Name of YHWH and means "gift of

Yah".

65   Moore, Philip, The End of History Messiah Conspiracy, Rameshead Press 1996.

66   *The Scriptures*, Institute for Scripture Research, (1998) p. 1216.

67   http://jacksonsnyder.com

68   Hellenism is generally defined as the cultural, linguistic and religious influence that the Greco-Roman era perpetuated throughout their empires. When I refer to Hellenistic influences in the context of the Walk in the Light series I am typically referring to the polytheistic and pagan aspects which flourished within the Hellenistic culture and pervaded society when the Messiah ministered on the Earth. This is the setting within which the Apostle Shaul was writing and he was often dealing with Hellenistic influences that were invading the early Assembly of Believers.

69   Having a relationship with the Messiah involves not only knowing His Name, but also obeying His commandments (1 Yahanan 2:3-6). He is the "Word made flesh" (Yahanan 1:14). The Word is His covenant and His Commands which are found in the Torah (Tehillim 105:8; 119). Therefore, if you desire a relationship with the Messiah you must obey the Torah, which He writes on your heart. (Devarim 6:6, Yirmeyahu 31:33). This is in direct contradiction to common Christian teaching which professes that the Torah (commonly mistranslated as "The Law") has been abolished and Believers are "under Grace." While a person is saved by grace, that does not mean that they spend the rest of their life in disobedience or lawlessness. Rather, they are saved from their lawless, sinful state by Grace and then they are expected to endeavor to live a righteous life under the instruction, guidance and power provided by the Ruach Hakodesh (Holy, Set Apart Spirit). This subject is described in greater detail in the Walk in the Light Series book entitled "Law and Grace."

70   www.experiencefestival.com.

71   www.innvista.com citing *Legge, Frances. Forerunners and Rivals of Christianity. 1964 and Koster, C.J. Come Out of Her My People. 1998.*

72   www.iaushua.com

73	ibid.
74	www.maitreya.org
75	The doctrine of baptism is often thought to be something new to the religious scene and uniquely Christian but according to the Scriptures Yahushua never Baptized anyone with water and John the Baptist (Yahanan the Immerser) was not a Christian. In actuality, Baptism is nothing new and was commanded by YHWH long before Messiah came. "Baptisms in the sense of purifications were common in the Old Testament. The "divers washings" (Greek "baptisms") are mentioned in Hebrews 9:10, and "the doctrine of baptisms," Hebrews 6:2. The plural "baptisms" is used in the wider sense, all purifications by water; as of the priest's hands and feet in the laver outside before entering the tabernacle, in the daily service (Exodus 30:17-21); of the high priest's flesh in the holy place on the day of atonement (Leviticus 16:23); of persons ceremonially unclean (Leviticus 14; 15; 16:26-28; 17:15; 22:4-6), a leper, one with an issue, one who ate that which died of itself, one who touched a dead body, the one who let go the scapegoat or buried the ashes of the red heifer, of the people before a religious festival (Exodus 19:10; John 11:55). The high priest's consecration was threefold: by baptism, unction, and sacrifice (Exodus 29:4; 40:12-15; Leviticus 8:1). "Baptism" in the singular is used specially of the Christian rite." (from Fausset's Bible Dictionary, Electronic Database Copyright (c)1998 by Biblesoft). It was a natural and significant thing for Yisra'elites to purify themselves through immersion. The Hebrew word for baptize is tevila (טביל) which is a full body immersion that takes place in a mikvah (מקוה) which comes from the passage in Beresheet 1:10 when YHWH "gathered together" the waters. The mikvah is the gathering together of flowing waters. To qualify as a mikvah, the waters must be living waters, they must be moving and they must contain life. It is interesting that Yahanan immersed people in the Yarden (Jordan) River which is a living water that flows into the Dead Sea which is literally dead. There is no life in the Dead Sea so it is not a mikvah, as if the sins of the people literally washed into the Sea of Death. There were numerous

Mikvahs at the temple and it was required that a person be immersed in a mikvah prior to presenting their sacrifice. Therefore, the tevila or baptism was common and full of meaning for a Yisra'elite and not some new initiation rite created by Christianity.

76 Yahuhanan (יהוחנן) is a name which means "YHWH has given." The Disciple who is commonly called John is often called Yohanan (יוחנן) but that loses the Name of YHWH. According to McClintock and Strong it is "a contracted form of the name JEHOHANAN." Therefore, in an effort to keep the original flavor of the name I use Yahonatan, Yahuhanan or Yahanan when referring to the Hebrew Disciple traditionally called John.

77 Kepha (כיפא) is the proper Hebrew transliteration for the Disciple who is commonly called Peter. His name means "a rock."

78 Yehezqel (יהזקאל) is the proper transliteration for the prophet commonly called Ezekiel. His name means "El will strengthen."

79 After reading this passage many Christians might object by saying: "Jesus told us not to swear at all." After all doesn't he tell us in Matthew 5:34 "not to swear at all." This is where we see a distinct difference between the Greek manuscripts and the Hebrew manuscripts. The Greek manuscripts describe the Messiah as changing the commandments, which is impossible, while the Hebrew manuscripts portray the Messiah as expounding the heart of the Torah and revealing the hypocrisy of the Pharisees, which is exactly what He came to do. In Devarim 6:13 we read: "You shall fear YHWH your Elohim and serve Him, and shall take oaths in His Name." Therefore, the Yisra'elites were actually commanded to swear in the Name of YHWH. It was common custom to swear and make oaths throughout the Tanakh (see Beresheet 24:2-3, 47:31; Joshua 2:12; 1 Shemuel 30:15; 2 Shemuel 19:7; 1 Kings 2:42; Ezra 10:5 to name a few). The Torah simply commands us not to swear falsely in the Name, nor profane the Name (Vayiqra 19:12). What happened was that men were

conniving that they could swear falsely so long as they did not do so in the Name of YHWH. Therefore they were swearing falsely by Heaven, Earth, Jerusalem etc. which they did not perceive to be a violation of the Torah. The Messiah was teaching that the Torah expected us to be honest in all our dealings and we were never to swear falsely, no matter what we swear by. He was not changing the Torah by forbidding the swearing of oaths rather He was teaching the full extent of the commandments. Ya'akov 5:12 merely affirms this teaching of the Messiah.

80 Hellenization was a process advanced by Alexander the Great which involved conquering nations and assimilating them into Greek civilization and imposing Greek customs upon them, while at the same time allowing the subjected people to remain somewhat autonomous and retain many of their customs and traditions. Often times the conquered nation would maintain its' individual characteristics while absorbing aspects of Greek culture, including the worship of many gods. This continued for hundreds of years and many of the early Believers of Yahushua lived within these Hellenized cultures. Many of the Gentile converts came out of these pagan cultures and as a result of this, along with the passage of time, many pagan concepts crept into the faith which has been perpetuated and compounded throughout the last two thousand years.

81 We are instructed in the Torah to wear tzit tzit (ציצת) on the four corners of our garments. (Bemidbar 15:38-39; Devarim 22:12). The Yahudim have traditionally fulfilled this instruction by wearing tallits which are also known as prayer shawls. Tefellim are also known as phylacteries and are worn in obedience to the Torah which instructs us to bind or tie the commandments on our hands and our foreheads. (Devarim 6:8; 11:18). Yahushua referred to both of these acts of obedience in Mattityahu 23:5 and criticized the manner in which the teachers of the Torah and the Pharisees obeyed because they did so to impress men – their hearts were not right. He did not say that we are not to obey the Torah and all children of Yisra'el should be following these instructions.

Doctrines such as "eternal security" that teach "once saved, always saved" are deceptive lies. They allow people to be lulled into complacency with the false assurance that everything will be alright so long as a simple prayer was said at some point in their life. The Scriptures teach us otherwise. It is how we live, not whether we said a prayer during a moment of clarity, weakness, despair or desperation. Everyone must come to the realization that they are tarnished by iniquity - that is the moment of truth. One can either repent from their transgressions or continue to live a life of lawlessness. Repentance can occur in a moment, but that decision must result in action which lasts for a lifetime. It is the process of turning away from a life of lawlessness and living a righteous life which involves obedience. We are told that if we love the Messiah we will obey His commandments. Thus we are to become His disciples. A disciple is not one who used to follow the Messiah, that would be a former disciple. Rather, a disciple is one who follows and continues to follow. As Paul (Shaul) taught, we need to complete the race to receive the prize. (Acts 20:24; 1 Corinthians 9:24; 2 Timothy 4:7; Ibrim 12:1). If you quit the race or do not follow the track, you will either be disqualified or may never finish the race. In either case you will not receive your reward.

83 Shaul is the proper transliteration for the Hebrew name often spelled and pronounced as Paul.

84 There is no question that the Elohim of Yisra'el has presented Himself in a plural form, but this is largely due to the fact that we presently exist in a four dimensional world and YHWH is not a four dimensional Being. He transcends our present state of physical existence and is not subject to time. Thus He describes Himself in multiple dimensions, but this does not mean that He is three separate entities.

85 Tehillim 138:2 New International Version.

Appendix A

Tanakh Hebrew Names

Torah - Teaching

English Name	Hebrew	English Transliteration
Genesis	בראשית	Beresheet
Exodus	שמות	Shemot
Leviticus	ויקרא	Vayiqra
Numbers	במדבר	Bemidbar
Deuteronomy	דברים	Devarim

Nebi'im - Prophets

Joshua	יהושע	Yahushua
Judges	שופטים	Shoftim
Samuel	שמואל	Shemu'el
Kings	מלכים	Melakhim
Isaiah	ישעיהו	Yeshayahu
Jeremiah	ירמיהו	Yirmeyahu
Ezekiel	יחזקאל	Yehezqel
Daniel	דניאל	Daniel
Hosea	הושע	Hoshea
Joel	יואל	Yoel
Amos	עמוס	Amos
Obadiah	עבדיה	Ovadyah

Jonah	יונה	Yonah
Micah	מיכה	Mikhah
Nahum	נחום	Nachum
Habakkuk	חבקוק	Habaquq
Zephaniah	צפניה	Zepheniyah
Haggai	חגי	Chaggai
Zechariah	זכריה	Zekaryah
Malachi	מלאכי	Malachi

Kethubim – Writings

Psalms	תהלים	Tehillim
Proverbs	משלי	Mishle
Job	איוב	Iyov
Song of Songs	שיר השירים	Shir ha-Shirim
Ruth	רות	Ruth
Lamentations	איכה	Eikhah
Ecclesiastes	קהלת	Qohelet
Esther	אסתר	Ester
Ezra	עזרא	Ezra
Nehemiah	נחמיה	Nehemyah
Chronicles	דברי הימים	Divri ha-Yamim

Appendix B

The Walk in the Light Series

Book 1   Restoration – A discussion of the pagan influences
          that have mixed with the true faith through the ages
          which has resulted in the need for restoration. This
          book also examines true Scriptural restoration.

Book 2   Names – Discusses the True Name of the Creator
          and the Messiah as well as the significance of names
          in the Scriptures.

Book 3   The Scriptures – Discusses the origin of the written
          Scriptures as well as many translation errors which
          have led to false doctrines in some mainline
          religions.

Book 4   Covenants – Discusses the progressive covenants
          between the Creator and His Creation as described
          in the Scriptures which reveals His plan for
          mankind.

Book 5   The Messiah – Discusses the prophetic promises
          and fulfillments of the Messiah and the True
          identity of the Redeemer of Yisra'el.

Book 6   The Redeemed – Discusses the relationship between
          Christianity and Judaism and reveals how the
          Scriptures identify True Believers. It reveals how the
          Christian doctrine of Replacement Theology has
          caused confusion as to how the Creator views the
          Children of Yisra'el.

Book 7   The Law and Grace – Discusses in depth the false
          doctrine that Grace has done away with the Law and
          demonstrates the vital importance of obeying the
          commandments.

Book 8	The Sabbath – Discusses the importance of the Seventh Day Sabbath as well as the origins of the tradition concerning Sunday worship.
Book 9	Kosher – Discusses the importance of eating food prescribed by the Scriptures as an aspect of righteous living.
Book 10	Appointed Times – Discusses the appointed times established by the Creator, often erroneously considered to be "Jewish" holidays, and critical to the understanding of prophetic fulfillment of the Scriptural promises.
Book 11	Pagan Holidays – Discusses the pagan origins of some popular Christian holidays which have replaced the Appointed Times.
Book 12	The Final Shofar – Discusses the walk required by the Scriptures and prepares the Believer for the deceptions coming in the End of Days.

The series began as a simple Power point presentation which was intended to develop into a book with twelve different chapters but ended up being twelve different books. Each book is intended to stand alone although the series was originally intended to build from one section to another. Due to the urgency of certain topics, the books have not been published in sequential order.

For anticipated release dates, announcements and additional teachings go to:
www.shemayisrael.net

Appendix C

The Shema

Deuteronomy (Devarim) 6:4-5

Hear, O Israel: The LORD our God, the LORD is one!
You shall love the LORD your God with all your heart,
with all your soul, and with all your strength.

Traditional English Translation

שְׁמַע יִשְׂרָאֵל יְהוָה אֱלֹהֵינוּ יְהוָה אֶחָד

וְאָהַבְתָּ אֵת יְהוָה אֱלֹהֶיךָ בְּכָל־ לְבָבְךָ וּבְכָל־ נַפְשְׁךָ וּבְכָל־ מְאֹדֶךָ

Modern Hebrew Text

Ancient Hebrew Text

Shema, Yisra'el: YHWH Elohenu, YHWH echad!
V-ahavta et YHWH Elohecha b-chol l'vavcha u-v-chol
naf'sh'cha u-v-chol m'odecha.

Hebrew Text Transliterated

Appendix D

Shema Yisrael

Shema Yisrael was originally established with two primary goals: 1) The production and distribution of sound, Scripturally based educational materials which would aid individuals to find and Walk in the Light of Truth. This first objective was, and is, accomplished through Shema Yisrael Publications; and 2) The free distribution of those materials to the spiritually hungry throughout the world along with Scriptures, food and clothing for the poor, the needy, the widow, the orphan, the sick, the dying and those in prison. This second objective was accomplished through the Shema Yisrael Foundation and through the Foundation people were able to receive a tax deduction for their contributions.

Sadly, through the Pension Reform Act of 2006 Congress severely restricted the operation of donor advised funds which, in essence, crippled the Shema Yisrael Foundation by requiring that funds either be channeled through another Foundation or to a 501 (c)(3) organization approved by the IRS. Since we operated very "hands on" by putting cash and materials directly into the hands of the needy in Third World Countries, we were unable to effectively continue operating the Foundation with the tax advantages associated therewith.

Therefore, Shema Yisrael Publications has effectively functioned in a dual capacity to insure that both objectives continue to be promoted, although contributions are no longer tax deductible. To review some of the work being accomplished you can visit www.shemayisrael.net and go to the "Missions" section.

To donate, make checks payable to: Shema Yisrael Publications and mail to:

Shema Yisrael
123 Court Street •Herkimer, New York 13350

You may also call (315) 939-7940 to make a donation
or receive more information.